PROVE IT

DEFEND THE CHRISTIAN FAITH

DR. STEPHEN CUTCHINS

foreword by

DR. NORMAN GEISLER

SECOND EDITION

Auxano Press
Tigerville, South Carolina
www.AuxanoPress.com

ISBN: 978-1-5087-2564-0

Published by Auxano Press
Tigerville, South Carolina
www.AuxanoPress.com

ENDORSEMENTS

"This helpful guide hits home with the Millennial generation."
George Barna and Jimmy Meyers, Co-Authors
Fearless Parenting: How to Raise Faithful Kids in a Secular Culture

"*Prove It* by Stephen Cutchins is one of the best written, best organized, and most timely books to fill the need to provide a defense for our faith. Never has the evangelical church needed books like this more than today. Every pastor, every parent, every Sunday School teacher, and every youth worker needs this book. I highly recommend it."
Dr. Norman Geisler, Distinguished Senior
Professor of Theology and Apologetics
Southern Evangelical Seminary - Charlotte, NC

"May I recommend to you Stephen Cutchins's book, *Prove It*. Doctrinally sound and practical in application, this book is a well-grounded defense of the gospel and will encourage you in your faith. I pray it will help you grow in the Lord Jesus and be a strong witness for Him."
Frank S. Page, Ph.D., President and Chief Executive Officer,
Executive Committee of the Southern Baptist Convention

"*Prove it* will help you understand and explain your faith. It is a unique book that can be used for small group study or as a stand alone read. I highly recommend it."
Dr. Ken Hemphill, Special Assistant to the President
for Denominational Relations
North Greenville University - Tigerville, SC

"Dr. Cutchins has done the Lord's Church a great service by writing *Prove It*, which provides Christians at all levels the knowledge and understanding they need to share their Christian faith confidently and persuasively with seekers and skeptics alike. It is rare to find a book that is both tremendously informative and accessible for both the newest of believers and the most mature Christians alike. *Prove It* is just such a book. Every Christian will benefit greatly from reading and re-reading *Prove It*. We are proud to have Dr. Cutchins as an SES alumnus."

Dr. Richard Land, President
Southern Evangelical Seminary - Charlotte, NC

"When the first edition of *Prove It* was published in 2015, we gave away a few thousand copies as our gift to everyone on Easter Sunday. Our people loved it. I then invited the author, my friend, Dr. Stephen Cutchins, to teach it on 7 consecutive Sunday nights. The room was packed every night! This book is exactly what today's church members are looking for. It offers practical help in defending the faith in a skeptical culture."

Dr. J. Kie Bowman, Senior Pastor
Hyde Park Baptist/The Quarries Church - Austin, TX

"*Prove It* is a foundational text for the apologetics courses at Fruitland Baptist Bible College. This excellent book is not only a wonderful resource for ministerial students, it is a great book for all Christians who desire to defend the faith. It is my hope that those who are skeptical about the claims of Christianity will also read this compelling book and place saving faith in the Lord Jesus Christ. Getting *Prove It* into the hands of those who are not yet believers can be a powerful evangelism tool!"

Dr. David B. Horton, President
Fruitland Baptist Bible College - Hendersonville, NC

"The topic of theology and apologetics can be overwhelming. Not so with *Prove It!* Stephen Cutchins has taken the complex and made it accessible for anyone investigating Christianity or wanting to make sense of the difficult questions of faith. I recommend this book as a valuable tool for the local church."

Dr. Ryan Pack, Senior Pastor
Riverland Hills Baptist Church - Columbia, SC

"Prove It by Stephen Cutchins is one of the best surveys of apologetics that you'll ever find. It is solidly biblical, extremely readable, and immensely practical. I used the book in a course I taught on Christian Apologetics in the Graduate School of Ministry at Dallas Baptist University. The students loved it! Stephen's online supplemental curriculum materials are a real bonus and invaluable resources for any classroom or small group study setting."

Dr. Jim Lemons, Professor of Theological Studies and Leadership
Dallas Baptist University - Dallas, TX

"Stephen Cutchins is one of the bright thinkers in the Church today. In *Prove It*, he's offered a straightforward way to explore and explain the most complex challenges of the Christian faith. His unique approach paves the way for a greater confidence in things of God – and that could change your life!"

Ryan Rush, Senior Pastor
Kingsland Baptist Church - Katy, TX

"If you are looking for a clear and easy to understand book on apologetics (how to defend your Christian faith), you should read *Prove It.* Stephen Cutchins has explained simply what we need to know, with many excellent illustrations. Check out the table of contents."

Dr. Thomas L. Constable, Senior Professor
Emeritus of Bible Exposition
Dallas Theological Seminary - Dallas, TX

DEDICATION

I dedicate this book to my wife, Wendy Cutchins. She is an amazing woman and I thank God for her everyday. Without her support and encouragement, this book would not be a reality.

Note:

There is a free small group curriculum for this book at

www.StephenCutchins.com

CONTENTS

ACKNOWLEDGEMENTS

First, I want to thank the people of First Baptist Church of North Augusta, SC for their amazing support of me and my family. For over five years, Wendy and I prayed that God would prepare me to serve as a Senior Pastor, and that He would also prepare a church for me to serve. You are that church. It is the highlight of my career to serve as your Senior Pastor.

I also want to thank Dr. J. Kie Bowman, Senior Pastor of Hyde Park Baptist Church in Austin, TX, for his support in getting the first edition of this book published in 2015. I am thankful to God for connecting the two of us for an exciting season of ministry and for teaching me the importance of prayer through our time together.

I would also like to thank Dr. Ken Hemphill for his vision for publishing works like this one with the goal of helping churches grow. I first met Dr. Hemphill while serving at First Baptist Church of Hendersonville, NC. During my time there, he was an active member of the church and was very supportive of my ministry.

For many years, Dr. Norman Geisler has been my mentor and teacher. He has always taken time to answer my questions and I would like to thank him for his support of this project. I cannot adequately describe what a joy it is to have him write the foreword to this book.

During my time as a student at Southern Evangelical Seminary, Dr. Barry Leventhal served as my teacher, mentor, and friend. I would like to thank him for providing rigorous instruction and insight. He encouraged me to go further than I thought possible.

In addition, I wish to thank the following people:

Wendy Cutchins: my wife and partner in life, who is a gift from God.

Madelyn and Sarah Cutchins; my daughters, who teach me how to be a Dad.

Jean Cutchins Parkhurst; my mother (living), who kept me from ever doubting that I am loved.

Dr. Fred L. Cutchins: my dad, who although he has passed away continues to inspire me in his absence.

FOREWORD

This is a great book! Surveys show that there is a mass exodus of young adults from our churches today. Sadly, they are departing largely because of doubts they have about the Bible. More sadly is that they acquired those doubts while they were in our Sunday Schools and Youth programs!

The famous preacher, Charles Spurgeon, identified the problem over a hundred years ago: We are entertaining the goats while we should be feeding the sheep.

When I was asked some time ago what we need to do, in line with Spurgeon, I added: "We should stop entertaining our young people and start training them."

Training them in what? In apologetics and theology. Very simply, the church has been remiss in training its youth in *what* we believe (theology) and *why* we believe it (apologetics).

I am often asked how I got involved in apologetics some 60 years ago. The answer is simple: while witnessing for Christ, I was asked questions I could not answer. I concluded that I was either going to have to get answers or else stop witnessing.

The turning point came early in my Christian experience. After being stumped by several cultists, I was challenged by a drunk in a Detroit ghetto to stop witnessing because, as he pointed out in my red-letter edition of the Bible, Jesus Himself told the disciples to "Go and tell no man." I had no idea what that verse meant, but there it was in bright red letters in my Bible. I had to make a decision: either stop witnessing or get answers.

I dedicated the next twenty years of my life to getting answers and the following forty years to writing them down. Many of these answer books I wrote are found in the footnotes of this excellent book by Dr. Stephen Cutchins.

Perhaps the greatest apologist of the 20th century was C. S. Lewis. In addition to his many excellent children's books (like *The Chronicles of Narnia*), he wrote great apologetic books (like *Mere Christianity, The Problem of Pain,* and *Miracles*). One short citation from his book *The Weight of Glory* (p. 50) summarizes the situation well: "To be ignorant and simple now—not to be able to meet the enemies on their own ground—would be to throw down our weapons, and to betray our uneducated brethren who have, under God, no defense but us against the intellectual attacks of the heathen. Good philosophy must exist, if for no other reason, because bad philosophy needs to be answered."

Prove It by Dr. Stephen Cutchins is one of the best written, best organized, and most timely books to fill the need posed by C.S. Lewis. Never has the evangelical church needed books like this more than today. Every pastor, every parent, every Sunday School teacher, and every youth worker needs this book. I highly recommend it.

BY DR. NORMAN GEISLER

INTRODUCTION

Prove it.

This is the cry of a generation that is both skeptical of truth and hostile toward Christianity. Too many people are turning away from Christianity, and God, because they have questions and challenges that go unanswered. Because of this, Christianity is viewed by many as an insanity that is only for the weak-minded and misguided. The purpose of this book is to introduce the basic concepts, contenders, and criticisms of Christianity and prepare the reader to provide a defense for the hope that is in them (1 Peter 3:15).

The importance of this book, and others like it, cannot be overstated from both a practical and an academic sense. The local church has a serious responsibility to defend the basic concepts of the Christian faith but cannot keep up with the attacks without basic tools and training that will equip Christians to love people enough to answer their hard questions.

Unless the church is equipped to deal with the intellectual mind that is rejecting the existence of God, the objective nature of truth, and the validity of miracles, a generation will be lost to the lies and confusion of false teaching. This book will enhance the readers' potential in the areas of apologetics (pre-evangelism) and evangelism.

My passion for apologetics started years ago when I was serving as a part-time youth pastor and teaching in the public schools in the Charlotte, NC area. I found that my students had questions about God and the Christian faith that I was not prepared to answer. After teaching for a few weeks out of a book for youth on Christian apologetics, I noticed that one of the authors, Dr. Norman Geisler, lived in Charlotte.

I nervously contacted him and offered to take him out to lunch to meet him. I assumed that he would graciously decline. To my surprise, he agreed to meet me for lunch and I think he even paid. Shortly after that, I began to study under him at Southern Evangelical Seminary and the rest is history.

It is a great joy to have Dr. Geisler write the foreword to this book. Much of what is presented in the pages that follow are directly influenced by, and borrowed from, my time learning from him in the classroom, at his home, and through his books. Dr. Geisler is a teacher and mentor who has always taken time to answer my questions.

What follows is a reformatted version of my doctoral dissertation, which was originally designed to be an eight-week curriculum. As you read, let me encourage you to stick it out to the end. **The payoff for all your reading will come in chapter seven** as all the information culminates with a discussion of evil, pain, and suffering.

OBJECTIVES

*"But sanctify the Lord God in your hearts, and always **be ready to give a defense** to everyone who asks you a reason for the hope that is in you, with meekness and fear"* (1 Peter 3:15).

Prove It covers nineteen educational objectives that are split into three big ideas covered in three sections. The three sections are titled "The Big Concepts," "The Big Contenders," and "The

Big Criticisms." "The Big Concepts" covers the truth about truth, God, and miracles. "The Big Contenders" covers the truth about world religions and cults. "The Big Criticisms" covers the truth about evil, pain, and suffering.

It is important to note that every chapter in this book is grounded in a healthy integration of theology and philosophy, including the interweaving of logic and reason into the objectives.

The following objectives are a comprehensive list of what the reader can expect to learn from reading this book. Although these objectives do not represent every concept covered in *Prove It*, it is reasonable to expect that every reader who completes this book should be able to achieve them. The objectives are:

1. Define *Christian apologetics*.

2. Explain why Christian apologetics is important.

3. Define *truth*.

4. Evaluate this statement: "Christianity is true for you but not for me."

5. Defend this statement: "The Bible is wholly true in all it affirms."

6. List three reasons, other than the Bible, why we know God exists.

7. List the three major worldviews.

8. Explain how we understand Jesus is God.

9. Explain why this statement is false: "Christians claim they worship one God, but they actually worship three: Jesus, the Holy Spirit, and God the Father."

10. Define *miracle*.

11. List three reasons miracles are critical to Christianity.

12. Describe three characteristics of a world religion.

13. List the four major world religions.

14. From a Christian perspective, define *cult*.

15. Describe three ways cults differ from Christianity.

16. Explain the differences between a world religion and a cult.

17. Answer this question: "If God is good, why did He create evil?"

18. Explain why God allows painful things to happen.

19. Explain how you would answer a friend who asked you to give a Christian answer to the argument below:

    • If God is all-good, He would destroy evil.

    • If God is all-powerful, He could destroy evil.

    • But evil is not destroyed.

    • Therefore, there is no such God.

PHILOSOPHY

"And the things that you have heard from me among many witnesses, commit these to faithful men who will be able to teach others also" (2 Timothy 2:2).

Paul encouraged Timothy to pass on the things that he had been taught to faithful men who would be able to teach others (2 Timothy 2:2). In this one verse, there are four levels or generations of discipleship. The flow of information was intended to move from Paul (1) … to Timothy (2) … to faithful men able to teach (3) … to others (4). This is the same desire that Jesus had for His disciples (Matthew 28:19-20).

This type of second and third-level discipleship is what drives any philosophy of ministry that has significance in the Kingdom of God today. *Prove It* is also based on this model and the content presented in the following pages should be passed on to others. As you read, think of yourself as a **conduit** and not just a **collector** of information.

THOUGHTS ON CHRISTIAN EDUCATION

"Teaching is both a science and an art,"[1] and there is no lack of information about how and what a person should teach in any given subject area. However, it seems that few books answer the question of *why* a person should teach a given subject area. Many teachers completely miss the point when it comes to the purpose of teaching. This is especially true when it comes to Christian education and, more specifically, Christian apologetics.

This line of thinking (or perhaps lack of thinking) is what has led us to a place where the absence of effective Bible teaching and Christian apologetics is prevalent in the local church. Consequently, biblical illiteracy and ignorance has also become commonplace in our churches. Ironically, today's Christian educators and apologists have more technological tools for Bible study at their fingertips than in any previous generation, yet less wisdom than ever about how to take it in, process it, and distribute it. Apathy and laziness have developed around the teaching, learning, and defending of even the most basic Bible truths.

Teaching is Part of Christian Growth

Teaching and defending the truths of the Bible is essential because it is part of growing as a Christian. As a Christian grows, he or she should be in the process of changing. It is important

---

[1] Howard Hendricks, *Teaching to Change Lives* (Sisters, OR: Multnomah, 1987), 51.

to remember that the job of the teacher is dynamic and should be constantly developed, evaluated, and refined. Paul writes that Christians are to be transformed by the renewing of their minds (Romans 12:1-2).

Long-time Bible teacher Howard Hendricks writes, "The law of the teacher, simply stated, is this: If you stop growing today, you stop teaching tomorrow."[2] God desires for His people to move through the process of sanctification and become more like Christ. Even Jesus Himself is recorded as having grown and developed from a boy to a man. Hendricks notes, "The more you change, the more you become an instrument of change in the lives of others."[3]

There is nothing more exciting and rewarding than a life that is changing as a result of being dedicated to God and His will. "What were we made for? To know God. What aim should we set for our lives? To know God. What is the 'eternal life' that Jesus gives? Knowledge of God. What is the best thing in life, bringing more joy, delight, and contentment, than anything else? Knowledge of God."[4] An individual who is growing in the knowledge of God will naturally begin to teach and instruct others as an outflow of growing closer to Him. Why does one teach? Because it is a part of growing as a Christian. What an honor to be used by God to communicate His message to a world that is constantly trying to ignore the Creator.

Jesus Modeled Teaching

To be like Jesus is to be a teacher. "Truly, without question, Jesus Christ was the Teacher par excellence!"[5] He is the one from whom disciples learn how to teach. He began to teach at a very

---

[2] Ibid., 17.
[3] Ibid., 21.
[4] J. I. Packer, *Knowing God* (Downers Grove: InterVarsity Press, 1973), 29.
[5] Ibid., 21.

young age and, even as a boy, amazed teachers of His day. As a man, He was commonly referred to as a rabbi and teacher. "If one wishes to teach, what better example is there than that of the greatest teacher, our Lord Jesus Christ?"[6] Believers should strive to emulate Christ's teaching, which focused on God the Father. "Every story has a central character around whom the action is built. In the Bible this character is God."[7] Jesus' way of teaching about God was specific to His audience. He spent time investing in a core group of disciples as well as preaching sermons to great multitudes from mountaintops.

Although we are to use Jesus as our model, we are also to realize that He had ultimate authority from the Father. "Our authority, however, is derived. Therefore, we cannot expect to duplicate Jesus in receiving words directly from the Father, in having innate, complete knowledge of what others were thinking, in the unparalleled absoluteness of His claims, and in exercising the sovereign authority of His commands."[8] However, under this authority, Jesus charged His followers to continue His teaching mission. To be like Jesus is to be a teacher.

Jesus Commissioned His Followers to Teach

Jesus left His followers with a very specific mission statement when He said, *"All authority has been given to Me in heaven and on earth. Go therefore and make disciples of all the nations, baptizing them in the name of the Father and of the Son and of the Holy Spirit, **teaching them** to observe all things that I have commanded you; and lo, I am with you always, even to the end of the age"* (Matthew 28:18-20).

---

[6] Roy B. Zuck, *Teaching as Jesus Taught* (Grand Rapids: Baker Books, 1995), 14.

[7] Jim Wilhoit and Ryken Leland, *Effective Bible Teaching* (Grand Rapids: Baker Book House, 1988), 186.

[8] Zuck, 57.

If Christians are to take seriously the charge to "make disciples," then they must be ready to teach people to obey all of Christ's commands. There are twelve different Old Testament words and seventeen different New Testament words for "teaching." Perhaps the best definition for teaching is simply, "to cause learning."

Paul, a master teacher, took the command to teach very seriously as illustrated by his charge to Timothy to pass on what he had received *"to faithful men who will be able to teach others also"* (2 Timothy 2:2). However, it is important to remember that in order to teach something one must first know the subject. Paul was able to teach only what he had already received from the Lord. "Personal ownership of what one teaches is the minimum requirement for effective Bible teaching."[9]

Teaching is Essential

The Bible holds the key to all of man's major needs in life, but it is important to remember that a teacher cannot force ideas into the minds of their students. The first step is to identify what the student perceives as a need in their life and begin there. As Wilhoit and Lel note, "We need to remind each other, therefore, that teachers can never do for students what they are unwilling to do for themselves."[10] However, it is also important for teachers to help guide students to identify their needs in a clearer way. This process is needed, but it is also very slow.

"Effective teachers have learned to travel slowly. They know that they often teach more by teaching less."[11] The ultimate goal of the Bible is to address a person's spiritual needs; that must be the goal of any Christian education program. "Whenever peo-

---

[9] Wilhoit and Ryken, *Effective Bible Teaching*, 27.
[10] Ibid., 45.
[11] Ibid., 47.

ple use the Bible for its intended purpose of spiritual and moral growth, they have achieved the main goal of Bible study."[12] It is also the job of the teacher to meet the spiritual needs of the student by rightly dividing the Word.

Paul was so passionate about this that when he wrote to the young and struggling pastor Timothy, he urged him to follow his example of "sound teaching" (2 Timothy 1:13, NIV). The value of sound teaching is very high, but the damage that poor teaching can do is very serious. There are many people in our churches today who are still struggling with basics like the simplicity of salvation by grace alone, through faith alone, in Christ alone (Ephesians 2:8-9) because they have been taught an unclear gospel that is not biblical. "The truth of the Gospel is simple, but never simplistic."[13] However, on the other side, there is no need to be paralyzed by perfectionism either. "Nothing would be done at all if man waited until he could do it so well that no one could find fault with it."[14]

We teach the truths of the Bible because it is part of growing as a Christian. Jesus modeled this for us in His life, and it is part of our purpose; there is a real need for it in this fallen world. C. S. Lewis said, "The first qualification for judging any piece of workmanship from a corkscrew to a cathedral is knowing what it is— what it was intended to do and how it was meant to be used."[15]

The ultimate goal of all Christian education is to cause godly life change in both the student and the teacher. No matter how many times a person teaches the Bible, it should always be fresh

---

[12] Ibid., 125.

[13] Marlene D. LeFever, *Creative Teaching Methods* (Elgin, IL.: D.C. Cook., 1985), 217.

[14] Ibid., 23.

[15] C.S. Lewis, *A Preface to Paradise Lost*, Oxford University Press Pbk Ed. (New York: Oxford University Press, 1961), 1.

and relevant. Every little nuance in the biblical text is an opportunity to pull out wisdom and truth. For this reason, it is important not to move too fast through the text. A hindrance to effective teaching is giving too much information at one time. In order to see life change in students, a teacher must be willing, and able, to evaluate what the student is actually learning.

Teaching that falls on deaf ears is really just talking. The challenge in the Christian education process is to unleash the Bible's potential to enlighten the student to things that they can learn from no other source, to expose the realities of the student's situation, and to equip the student to serve. This is the purpose of *Prove It*.

The Ultimate Objectives of Christian Education

What does the end result of effective Christian education look like? Are there certain concepts that are non-negotiable and that all Christian educators should commit to being held accountable to teaching? Why is it so difficult to get theologians, church leaders, and Christian educators to agree on the basic objectives of Christian education? Christian education should lead persons into:

1. A consciousness of God as the supreme reality in human experience, to a personal relationship with Him through Jesus Christ and to a sense of moral responsibility to Him (i.e., a theocentric view of reality).

2. An understanding and appreciation of the personality, life, and teachings of Jesus Christ; to an experience of Him as Savior from sin, Friend, Companion, and Lord; and a loyalty to Him in daily life and conduct (i.e., a lifelong commitment to discipleship

or following after Him in faith and obedience).

3. A knowledge and experience of the person and work of the Holy Spirit as Comforter, Teacher, Guide, and source of power (i.e., the spiritual life: life in the Spirit).

4. A knowledge, love, and effective use of the Bible as the inspired Word of God and the final authority in the faith and conduct (i.e., the devotional and ministering life).

5. An understanding and ongoing commitment to biblical stewardship under the lordship of Christ-involving time, talent, and treasure.

6. An appreciation of the nature and function of the Christian Church and to vital participation in its life and work—both as the gathered Church and the scattered Church (e.g., worship, teaching, equipping, service, fellowship, evangelism, etc.).

7. An appreciation of the meaning and importance of the Christian home and a commitment and ability to participate constructively in its life and responsibility.

8. A progressive and continuous development of Christ-like character (i.e., a biblically-based life of faith: spiritual, moral, mental, and social growth).

9. An enthusiastic and worthy participation in propagating the Gospel to the whole world (i.e., the Great Commission: the missionary mandate of the church).

10. **An understanding and commitment to the Christlike vocation of suffering in a world of**

alienation and pain (i.e., the ultimate call as a servant of Christ).

11. An intelligent and scriptural participation as a Christian citizen in the community, state, and world (i.e., the ongoing lifestyle of a world-Christian).

12. A biblical/Christian interpretation of life and the universe, and a commitment to a philosophy of life built on the interpretation (i.e., a theistic/Trinitarian worldview).[16]

Prove It honors each of these objectives, but is structured to bring special attention to Objective 10. When first introduced to this list, Objective 10 stands out as being a commonly neglected area of contemporary Christian education. Most of what makes up popular Christian education literature today is targeted at making people feel good and falls short in teaching about the "Christlike vocation of suffering in a world of alienation and pain."[17]

As a response to this, *Prove It* is dedicated to helping readers understand the suffering that is encountered in this world full of evil and pain. Christian Apologetics may be simply defined as the **defense of the Christian faith**. We should do apologetics because **reason demands it** and the **Bible commands it**.

TEN BIBLICAL REASONS WHY WE DO APOLOGETICS

1. We are commanded to **defend** the Christian faith. *"But sanctify Christ as Lord in your hearts, always being ready to make a defense to everyone who asks you to give an account for the hope that is in you, yet with gentleness and reverence"* (1 Peter 3:15,

---

[16] Howard Hendricks, *CE809: Teaching Techniques* [Class Handout] (Charlotte: Southern Evangelical Seminary, 2010).
[17] Ibid.

NASB).

2. We are commanded to **refute** false ideas about God. *"We are destroying speculations and every lofty thing raised up against the knowledge of God, and we are taking every thought captive to the obedience of Christ"* (2 Corinthians 10:5, NASB).

3. We are commanded to **discern** true from false prophets. *"Beloved, do not believe every spirit, but test the spirits to see whether they are from God, because many false prophets have gone out into the world"* (I John 4:1, NASB).

4. Jesus **corrected** error. *"But Jesus answered and said to them, you are mistaken, not understanding the Scriptures nor the power of God"* (Matthew 22:29, NASB).

5. Jesus **rejected** false teachings. *"This people honors Me with their lips, but their heart is far away from Me. But in vain do they worship Me, teaching as doctrines the precepts of men"* (Matthew 15:8-9, NASB).

6. Paul **reasoned** with people. *"But Saul kept increasing in strength and confounding the Jews who lived at Damascus by proving that this Jesus is the Christ"* (Acts 9:22, NASB).

7. Paul **refuted** those who opposed the truth. *"Holding fast the faithful word which is in accordance with the teaching, so that he will be able both to exhort in sound doctrine and to refute those who contradict"* (Titus 1:9, NASB).

8. Paul **rebuked** those in error. *"This testimony is true. For this reason reprove them severely so that they may be sound in the faith"* (Titus 1:13, NASB).

9. Paul **defended** the gospel. *"For it is only right for me to feel this way about you all, because I have you in my heart, since both in my imprisonment and in the defense and confirmation of the gospel, you all are partakers of grace with me"* (Philippians 1:7, NASB).

10. Jude urged that we **contend** for the faith. *"Beloved, while I was making every effort to write you about our common salvation, I felt the necessity to write to you appealing that you contend earnestly for the faith which was once for all handed down to the saints"* (Jude 3 NASB).

PART ONE:

THE BIG CONCEPTS

CHAPTER 1

THE TRUTH ABOUT TRUTH

What is truth?

Jesus said to him, "I am the way, <u>the truth</u>, and the life. No one comes to the Father except through Me" (John 14:6).

How does it make you feel when someone disagrees with you? If we are honest, it is probably a little natural to get irritated. One leadership thought is: "If you and your friend always agree, one of you is unnecessary." Having different perspectives can help you discover the truth in many situations.

Truth is telling it like it is. Truth can be described as "that which corresponds to reality." Contrary beliefs are possible, but contrary truths are not possible. We can believe everything is true, but we cannot make everything true. Truth accurately expresses an actual state of affairs and opposite ideas cannot both be true at the same time and in the same sense.

Some believe there is no truth at all or that truth cannot be known. However, this is a self-defeating position. A person may say: "There is no Truth." The problem: Is that a true statement? Both what is true and what is error CAN BE known and understood. Truth is like a mirror showing us how things really are. Things are not true simply because they "work." Cheating on a test may get you a good grade, but that grade does not represent the truth of what you have learned. Truth is also not simply what makes you feel good. A bad report from the doctor might cause you to feel bad, but it represents the truth. Truth is not always what you want to hear, but truth is valuable.

ALWAYS AN AUDIENCE

You may have noticed that some of the most popular people in this world are not sharing and living the truth. They have a large audience of people who are being influenced by them. It would be easy, and perhaps natural, to give credibility to people who have a large audience.

However, popularity is not the test of authenticity. Even in our churches, we should be mindful to not sacrifice truth in order to draw and maintain a larger audience. What God says about His Son is of greater authority than what any man may say. When we say what God says about Jesus, we are truthful. Anyone who does not, calls God a liar. We must agree to disagree with anything or anyone that opposes God's truth.

Consider these words written by Paul to the younger Timothy. *"For the time is coming when people will not endure sound teaching, but having itching ears they will accumulate for themselves teachers to suit their own passions, and will turn away from listening to the truth and wander off into myths"* (2 Timothy 4:3-4, ESV). Jesus also spoke about this matter. *"Enter by the narrow gate. For the gate is wide and the way is easy that leads to destruction, and those who enter by it are many. For the gate is narrow and the way is hard that leads to life, and those who find it are few"* (Matthew 7:13-14, ESV).

ABSOLUTE TRUTH

Absolute truth is true … for all people … at all times … in all places. Christianity is not just true for Christians, it is true for everyone. It is not just true subjectively, but it is true objectively. "Objective Truth" and "Absolute Truth" are the same. "Relative Truth" and "Subjective Truth" are also the same. Subjective, or relative truth is something true for SOME people, not for ALL people … or in SOME places, not ALL places … or at SOME times, not at ALL times. Truth is OBJECTIVE and ABSOLUTE not RELATIVE or SUBJECTIVE.

If two people say opposite things, they cannot both be true. One can be right and the other wrong, or they can both be wrong, but they cannot both be right. Once truth is discovered, anything that contradicts that truth can then be identified as a lie.

PROBLEMS WITH RELATIVE TRUTH

Relativism is actually self-defeating. Most relativists believe that relativism is true for everybody and not just them. How can it be true for everyone that nothing is true for everyone? They believe that it is absolutely true for everyone that truth is only relatively true for them.

Relativism is also full of contradictions. If a person says there is milk in the refrigerator and another insists there is no milk in the refrigerator, then there must be and not be milk in the refrigerator. God exists and God does not exist exhaust the only possibilities so one of them must be true and the other false.

Relativism also means that no one has ever been wrong about anything. No one can ever be wrong, even if he is! He is right even when he is wrong. However, the law of non-contradiction helps us understand that the opposite of true is FALSE. The law

5

of non-contradiction is undeniable. Even those who deny it use it.

Avicenna, the Great Medieval Philosopher, said that "Anyone who denies the law of non-contradiction should be beaten and burned until he admits that to be beaten is <u>not</u> the same as <u>not</u> to be beaten, and to be burned is <u>not</u> the same as <u>not</u> to be burned." The Law of Non-Contradiction is your greatest tool in answering postmodernism. To use it, just apply the claim to itself. Below, are few examples of these types of self-defeating statements.

Statement: "There is no truth."
Response: "Is that true?"

Statement: "Truth is relative."
Response: "Is that true for everyone?"

Statement: "You can't know truth."
Response: "How do you know that?"

Statement: "There are no absolutes."
Response: "Is that absolutely true?"

Statement: "Truth can't be trusted."
Response: "Should I trust that?"

Statement: "You ought not judge."
Response: "Is that a judgment?"

Statement: "The reader determines the meaning."
Response: "Should I determine the meaning of that statement?"

THE TRUTH ABOUT TRUTH

- All truth claims are absolute, narrow and exclusive. Even the claim that "every religion is true" excludes its opposite.

- Truth is discovered, not invented. It exists independent of anyone's knowledge of it. Gravity existed prior to Newton.

- Beliefs cannot change a fact, no matter how sincerely they are held. A person can sincerely believe the world is flat but that only makes them sincerely mistaken.

- Truth is trans-cultural. 2+2=4 here, there, and everywhere.

- Being raised in a given culture doesn't make the beliefs of that culture true or right. Becoming a Nazi while living in Nazi Germany doesn't make Nazism true or right.

- Truth is not affected by the attitude of the one professing it. An arrogant person does not make truth arrogant.

WHAT TRUTH IS NOT

- Truth is not what works. Cheating on a test may lead to a good grade but that grade does not accurately represent the truth of what you have learned.

- Truth is not what coheres. Although a chain and a web are cohesive, they cannot hang in "empty space." They must be anchored to something.

- Truth is not what was intended. When a person lies but intends to tell the truth … they still lie.

- Truth is not what is comprehensive. A person can have a "comprehensive" view of a lie or an incomplete view of truth.

- Truth is not what is relevant. A lie may connect with a person's feelings but not connect them with what is really happening.

- Truth is not what feels good. A bad report card may feel bad, but it represents the truth. Truth can produce bad feelings and lies can produce good feelings.

IS THE BIBLE TRUE?

There are actually two different questions that must be answered.

1. Do we have an accurate copy of the original New Testament documents?

2. Do the original New Testament documents tell the truth?

There is strong evidence for the reliability of the New Testament manuscripts. First is the number of New Testament manuscripts. There were nearly 5700 manuscripts of the New Testament, whereas a typical book of that time period would only have 7-10 copies. Second are the early dates (AD 117-138) of the New Testament production. No other book from the ancient world has this small of a time gap between composition and the earliest manuscripts. This is illustrated in the chart below.

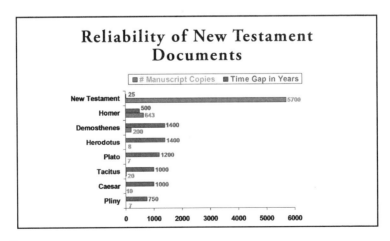

Third is the accuracy of the New Testament manuscripts. The Bible was more accurately copied than any other books from the ancient world. The accuracy of the New Testament has been estimated to be 99.9%. The Bible is the best known of any ancient book and there are 19,368 citations by the early fathers from the late first century onward. The illustration below visually displays how easily many variations in the text are resolved, despite not having the original manuscript available.

How do we know what the original said?

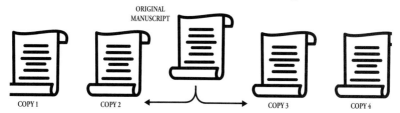

COPY 1: God is #ust and the jusitfier of the one who has faith in Jesus.
COPY 2: God is j#st and the jusitfier of the one who has faith in Jesus.
COPY 3: God is ju#t and the jusitfier of the one who has faith in Jesus.
COPY 4: God is jus# and the jusitfier of the one who has faith in Jesus.
ORIGINAL: God is just and the jusitfier of the one who has faith in Jesus.
Note: The NT Documents have *far fewer* variations than this example

JESUS IS THE KEY

In order to defend that the original New Testament documents tell the truth, we must acknowledge Jesus as the key. Jesus claimed and proved to be God by fulfilling prophecy, living a sinless and miraculous life, and predicting and accomplishing His resurrection from the dead. If Jesus is God, then anything He teaches is true.

JESUS AND THE OLD TESTAMENT

- Jesus Affirmed Its Divine Authority (Matthew 4:4; Matthew 4:10)

- Jesus Affirmed Its Imperishability (Matthew 5:17-18)
- Jesus Asserted Its Unbreakability (John 10:35)
- Jesus Declared Its Supremacy (Matthew 15:3,6)
- Jesus Affirmed Its Factual Inerrancy (Matthew 22:29)
- Jesus Insisted on Its Historical Reliability (Matthew 24:37-38; Matthew 12:40)
- Jesus Affirmed its Scientific Accuracy (Mark 13:19)

Because the New Testament was not yet written, Jesus' words apply directly only to the Old Testament. Jesus affirmed the scope of the Old Testament and promised the divine authority of the New Testament. The Old Testament was **directly** confirmed by Jesus to have divine authority and the New Testament was **indirectly** confirmed to have divine authority.

Why Truth Matters

Truth is telling it like it is. There are no relative truths. Things are either really true or really not true. There is nothing more important in our lives than our relationship to the one **true** God. John MacArthur writes: "We can have the happiness God gives; why should we settle for the cheap substitute Satan offers? We can have the success of living righteously and pleasing our heavenly Father; why should we settle for the brief and disappointing successes sin produces? By God's grace we can have the peace that passes understanding; why should we settle for the cheap satisfactions that everyone understands but that will soon pass?"

CHAPTER 2

THE TRUTH ABOUT GOD

HOW WE KNOW GOD EXISTS

There are three ways, other than reading the Bible, we can know God exists. The first is the beginning or **Cosmological Argument**. This argument basically says that anything that has a beginning has a beginner. Many scientists, including Albert Einstein, have concluded that the universe had a beginning. If the universe had a beginning, then it must have a Beginner.

The evidence leaves us with the following two options. Either no one created something out of nothing (the atheistic view) or Someone created something out of nothing (the theistic view). Which view is more reasonable? If you talk with an atheist, try asking them the following question: "If there is no God, why is there something rather than nothing at all?" God has always existed outside the universe and is infinitely powerful.

The second argument for God is the design or **Teleological Argument**, which states that anything that has a design has a designer. It is easy to see design in the biggest and smallest things in creation. The universe has design. The Anthropic Principle says that the average distance between stars in our galaxy is 30 trillion miles. That is the exact distance needed for earth to exist in its present life-supporting position.

DNA also has design. The DNA of one human cell has five million pages of information, which is equal to 25,000 two-hundred-page books. All of that is crammed into the nucleus of a cell. The width of a typical cell is about 1/10th the width of a human hair and you have about 100 TRILLION cells! If a house represented your little toe, baby peas that filled the house would represent the cells of your toe. And each of those peas would contain the information of 25,000 two-hundred-page books! God is infinitely intelligent and has purpose in His creation.

The third argument is the **Moral Argument**, which says if there is a moral law then there is a moral Lawgiver. In order to judge any action as either good or bad, we must have a gauge. If there is anything either morally good or morally bad in this world then there must be a moral gauge or law by which we decide. If there is a moral law then there must be a moral lawgiver. Was Hitler wrong? What about the rape of a child? How do you know? If there is one morally wrong thing, then God exists.

THE SEVEN WORLDVIEWS

A worldview is like a pair of glasses. You don't look at the glasses, you look through them. A worldview is a lens through which you see the world. There are seven basic worldviews. In each of the following images, the hand represents God and the world represents all of creation.

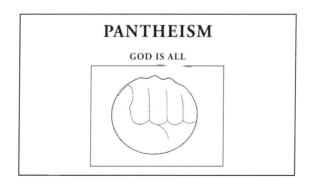

PANENTHEISM

GOD IS IN ALL

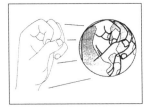

DEISM
GOD IS BEYOND THE WORLD
BUT NOT IN IT

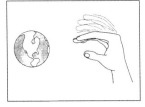

FINITE GODISM
GOD IS BEYOND THE WORLD
BUT IS LIMITED IN POWER/PERFECTION

Theism, Atheism, and Pantheism are the top three worldviews. Judaism, Islam and Christianity are proponents of a theistic worldview. The basic belief of Theism is that God created the world and that He sustains it. He is transcendent and does miracles other than creation. For the theist, God is in the world like a painter is in a painting, or a composer is in a composition.

Pantheism's basic belief is that God is all and all is God. Evil is not real and no miracles are possible. Proponents are Zen Buddhism and popular movies like *Star Wars* (The Force) and *Avatar* (Eywa).

The basic belief of atheism is that no God, infinite or finite, exists. For the atheist, evil exists and is evidence against God. No miracles are possible from an atheistic worldview. God is simply an illusion or projection.

"GOD IS _____"

"What comes into our minds when we think about God is the most important thing about us."[18] We can't know everything there is to know about God but we can **know God**. God is like

---

[18] A.W. Tozer, *The Knowledge of the Holy: The Attributes of God: Their Meaning in the Christian Life* (New York: Harper, 1961).

a rope that goes infinitely in both directions. You can hold it and see it but you can't see the ends. God has chosen to disclose Himself, and His self-disclosure is called revelation.

According to evangelical theology, God has revealed Himself in two ways: General Revelation (in His **world**) and Specific Revelation (in His **Word**). General Revelation is found in nature, man, history, art, and even music. Specific Revelation is found in the life of Jesus and the Bible. General Revelation is sufficient for condemnation but not salvation. Specific Revelation as contained in God's Word–both living (Jesus) and God's revealed message (as written in the Bible)–is necessary for salvation.

There are four important things about General Revelation. First, everybody knows it. Second, everybody understands it. Third, it has been happening since creation. Last, it is limited in revelation. General Revelation makes us responsible, but is not sufficient for justification. General revelation tells us only enough about God for **condemnation**. Specific Revelation tells enough about God for **salvation**.

"So then faith comes by hearing, and hearing by the word of God" (Romans. 10:17).

Biblical Support for General Revelation

"For since the creation of the world His invisible attributes are clearly seen, being understood by the things that are made, even His eternal power and Godhead, so that they are without excuse" (Romans 1:20).

"The heavens declare the glory of God; and the firmament shows His handiwork" (Psalms 19:1).

Biblical Support for Specific Revelation

"You search the Scriptures ... and these are they which testify of Me" (John 5:39).

"…Behold I have come—In the volume of the book it is written of Me…" (Hebrews 10:7).

"…He who has seen Me has seen the Father…" (John 14:9).

THE IMPORTANCE OF KNOWING GOD

Have you ever wondered what God is really like? What images come to mind when you think of God? We can't be like God unless we know what God is like. We can't know the true God unless we know the truth about God. We can't recognize false gods unless we know the true God.

We tend to become like the object we worship so it is important to know exactly who God is. The most important thing about us is what we think of God. An ultimate commitment to anything less than ultimate will not ultimately satisfy. We must guard our minds because idols are idols, whether they are mental or metal. The next section will go into great depth about who God is and what He does.

Attributes and Characteristics

It is important to differentiate between an "attribute" and a "characteristic" of God. Both are used to describe God, but they are slightly different in nature. An attribute is "an essential trait of God," whereas a characteristic "is simply something that belongs to God."[19] In other words, an attribute is what God is, independent of other things, whereas a characteristic of God is more a description of how He relates to His creation. For example, "without creation, God would have nothing to be sovereign over, transcendent in, or omnipresent to."[20]

There is also a difference between God's moral and nonmoral attributes or characteristics. Nonmoral attributes of God include

---

[19] Norman Geisler, *Systematic Theology, Volume 2: God, Creation.* (Minneapolis: Bethany House, 2003), 17, 20.
[20] Ibid., 21.

pure actuality, simplicity, aseity, necessity, immutability, externality, impassibility, infinity, immateriality, immensity, omnipotence, omnipresence, omniscience, wisdom, light, majesty, beauty, ineffability, life, immortality, unity, and triunity. Nonmoral characteristics of God include sovereignty, transcendence, and immanence. Moral attributes of God include holiness, justice, jealousy, perfection, truthfulness, and goodness (love). Moral characteristics of God include mercy and wrath.

Nonmoral Attributes and Characteristics

Pure actuality is "that which is (existence) with no possibility to not exist or to be anything other than it is—existence, pure and simple."[21] God is completely and totally everything that He could possibly be. In fact, this means that He also has no potential to be anything other than what He is.

Many of us are regularly on the Internet and one of the most familiar names on the Internet is Google. Google is the most-used search engine on the web today. Have you ever thought about what Google means? Actually, the term "Google" is a noun that became a verb.

You have most likely heard people saying "I Googled it." So Google is a verb. But what about "Google is one of the most popular search engines on the Internet"? Google is also a noun. Google is now used as both a noun and a verb.

God's name is also a verb—I AM. The verb tense here is imperfect and could be translated "I Am Who was, Who is, and Who will continue to be." God is completely and totally everything that He could possibly be. In fact, this means that He also has no potential to be anything other than what He is.

When it is said that a person has "no potential" it is generally not a positive statement and usually points to an inability to

---

[21] Ibid., 30.

grow to a higher level. However, in God's case, there is no potential because He actually is already at the highest level possible. Therefore, God having "no potential" is actually positive because it affirms His total completeness and lack of need (and ability) for any growth or change. I AM.

Simplicity means that God is without parts, indivisible, and absolutely one. "God is not capable of being divided."[22] One of the biggest struggles with this concept is a misunderstanding of the trinity of God's triunity. It is important to understand that there is only one *What* in God, even though there are three *Whos*.

Aseity denotes that God exists in and of Himself, independent of anything else. He is self-existent. However, this does not imply that God somehow created Himself because God is not created. He is the uncreated Creator and the uncaused Causer of all things. Closely related to aseity is God's **necessity**, which speaks to God's inability to not exist. His existence is essential.

Immutability means that God is unchangeable in His nature. God has nothing about His character or attributes that can change. To speak of God changing His mind or changing His will is simply wrong. *"God is not man, that he should lie, nor a son of man, that he should change his mind"* (Numbers 23:19 NIV).

Eternality means that God has no past, present, or future. He simply has the eternal present. Thus, God has the ability to see the future in a similar way to how we see the past. However, God does not just know the future and the past; He is actually present in all moments and is forever.[23]

Impassibility means that God cannot undergo passion or suffering; nothing in the created universe can make God feel pain or inflict misery on Him. God is capable of having feelings but

---

[22] Ibid., 39.
[23] Ibid., 58-93.

His feelings are not dependent on, or changed by, anything that happens in the world. God's **infinity** expresses that He is limitless in His being. He is without boundaries, a being beyond the limits of the created universe.

When explaining God's **immateriality**, it is important to understand that God is pure Spirit. This means that God is without a body or any material parts. Although there are many examples from Scripture that speak about God as having hands, eyes, or other bodily parts, these passages are not to be taken literally. **Immensity** means that God cannot be measured and is unlimited in extension.[24]

Omnipotence means that God has unlimited power. Although God is all-powerful, this does not mean that there aren't things that God cannot do. Whatever God does will be limited to His nature and will. God cannot do something that is in contradiction to His character. For example, God cannot lie (Titus 1:2). However, saying that God is unlimited in His ability to be truthful could state this idea positively.

An interesting question associated with this is, "Can God make a rock that He cannot pick up?" If the answer is yes, then it seems that the answer has limited God's power to pick up the rock. If the answer is no, then it appears that the answer has limited God's ability to create.

At first glance, either answer seems to contradict God's omnipotence. However, this is not true. The answer is no. God cannot make a rock that He cannot pick up, but this does not make God limited in power. In fact, God's inability to create something too big to be picked up actually affirms the power of God. What might appear to be weakness is actually unlimited strength. If the rock was too big for God to pick up, then the rock would be

---

[24] Ibid., 112-145.

bigger than God and would therefore be God. This simply cannot be.

Omnipresence means that there is no place where God is not. **Omniscience** and wisdom both speak to God's relationship to the truth. Omniscience affirms that God knows all things—past, present, and future. **Wisdom** is God's unerring ability to choose the right means to accomplish His will. It is the application of truth.

God is pure spiritual **light** (as opposed to physical light). God is light. He is the Great Illuminator—the Radiant One. He is also **majestic**. God's majesty consists of unsurpassed greatness, highest eminence, unparalleled exaltation, and unmatched glory.

Further, **beauty** is an essential element of majesty. It is the essential attribute of goodness that produces in the beholder a sense of overwhelming pleasure and delight. **Ineffability** means that God is incapable of being expressed. Theologically, it refers to the transcendent characteristics of God that cannot be adequately expressed in human language.[25]

Life and **immortality** are two attributes that express both the positive and negative qualities to God's existence. Life has two basic ideas: (1) God is alive, and (2) He is the source of all life. He has life intrinsically. He *is life*, while all other things *have life* as a gift from Him. God possesses life intrinsically and eternally. While life is what God has, immortality speaks to God's absence of death. It literally means "without death," "imperishable," and "incorruptible."

Unity literally means "oneness." There is one and only one God. There are not two or more gods. **Triunity** further says that there are three persons in one essence. God is three *Whos* in one *What*, a plurality within unity: Father, Son, and Holy Spirit.

---

[25] Ibid., 224-245.

Sovereignty is technically not an attribute, but an activity of God in relation to His creation. It is God's control over His creation, His governance over it, and His rule over all reality. **Transcendence** means that God is beyond the world. He is prior to all things, upholds all things, and is above all things. It is not an inherent trait of God, but a relational one.

Immanence literally means, "within" or "near." He is within or present in the entire universe. He is not within in the sense of being part of it, but He is in it as its sustaining Cause.[26]

Moral Characteristics and Attributes

Holiness combines both metaphysical and moral dimensions. Theologically, it means that He is totally and utterly apart from all creation and evil. Holiness also refers to His absolute moral uniqueness, as well as His total separateness from all creatures. **Justice** literally means, "To be just" or "right." Theologically, it refers to the intrinsic character of God wherein He is absolutely just or right, and is the ultimate standard of justice and rightness.[27]

The root meanings of the basic Old Testament word for "**jealous**" are "to be desirous of," "to be zealous about," "to be excited to anger over," and "to execute judgment because of." God has holy zeal to protect His supremacy and angry wrath over idolatry and other sins. While this may sound more like a characteristic, it is primarily an attribute. This is because God's jealousy is primarily over Himself.

It is right for God to be jealous over Himself because He is **perfect**. Perfection means flawless, excellent, complete, sound, blameless, without blemish, safe, entire, whole, and finished. God is **truthful**. Truth is telling it like it is. True statements cor-

---

[26] Ibid., 518-556.
[27] Ibid., 333.

respond to reality. Therefore, God is totally dependable. **Mercy** is "not getting what you deserve," a "ransom," or a "propitiatory" act. **Wrath** is a "burning anger" or an outburst of passion, anger, or rage.[28]

God is also **love**, which is one of God's best-known moral attributes. Love is defined as "willing the good of its object." For all practical purposes, "love" and "goodness" can be treated synonymously. Literally, the word "**omnibenevolent**" means "all-good." Agape is the highest kind of love. Although it is one of the most common words within the text of the New Testament, "agape" was actually not used much in other Greek writings of the time. The word "agape" is almost impossible to find apart from the New Testament. Perhaps this is because agape love is from God alone and is characterized by sacrifice. It is the power that motivates a person to respond to someone else's needs with no expectation of reward.

A LITTLE MORE ON THE TRINITY

The doctrine of the Trinity is based on two basic biblical teachings:

1. There is only one God.

2. There are three distinct persons who are God: the Father, the Son, and the Holy Spirit. God is one What and three Whos.

The Father is God.

- Jesus taught His disciples to pray to *"Our Father in heaven"* (Matthew 6:9).

- Paul said, *"There is but one God, the Father"* (1 Corinthians 8:6).

- God is referred to as the *"Father of our Lord Jesus*

---

[28] Ibid., 338-367.

Christ" (Romans 15:6).

The Son is God.

- Paul calls Jesus the One in whom *"the whole full-ness of deity dwells bodily"* (Colossians 2:9, ESV).
- In Titus, Jesus is called *"our great God and Savior"* (Titus 2:13).

The Holy Spirit is God.

- The Holy Spirit appears with the Father and Son in NT benedictions (2 Corinthians 13:14).
- The Holy Spirit appears in the baptism portion of the great commission (Matthew 28:18-20).

God is like a triangle. A triangle has **three** sides, but it is only **one** triangle. Take away any of the sides and it is not a triangle. In the same way, God is one What and three Whos. The image below shows this visually.

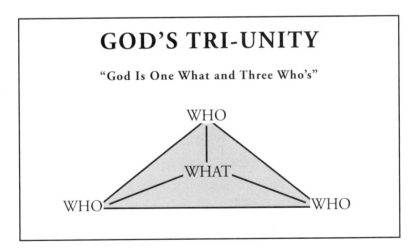

There are three persons in one God. God has a plurality of persons but a unity of essence; God is three persons in one nature. There is one "What" (essence) in God, but there are three "Whos" (persons) in that one What. God has three "I's" in His one "It". There are three subjects in the one object.

Polytheism holds that there are many finite gods beyond the world and in the world. Theism holds that there is one Infinite Personal God. This Christian view is not in contradiction with the doctrine of the trinity. The Hypostatic Union, the union of Christ's humanity and divinity in one hypostasis, is a mystery to be enjoyed. There is no way to deny that Jesus Christ was both God and man. Jesus was God in a human form.

The image below is a visual representation of Jesus as both God and man. The triangle represents God and the circle represents Christ's humanity. Notice that the triangle and the circle are touching but not overlapping. If they did overlap, you would have finite and infinite overlapping, which cannot logically happen. When *"Jesus increased in wisdom and stature, and in favor with God and men"* (Luke 2:52), it was the circle that grew and not the triangle. When Christ died on the cross and was buried, it was the circle not the triangle. God can't die.

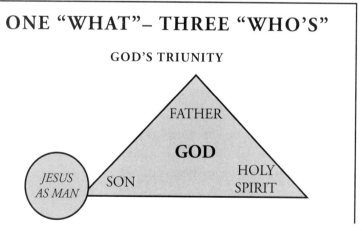

ONE "WHAT"– THREE "WHO'S"

GOD'S TRIUNITY

CHAPTER 3

THE TRUTH ABOUT MIRACLES

THE IMPORTANCE OF MIRACLES

How important do you think miracles are to Christianity?

"Now if Christ is preached that He has been raised from the dead, how do some among you say that there is no resurrection of the dead? But if there is no resurrection of the dead, then Christ is not risen.

"And if Christ is not risen, then our preaching is empty and your faith is also empty. *Yes, and we are found false witnesses of God, because we have testified of God that He raised up Christ, whom He did not raise up—if in fact the dead do not rise. For if the dead do not rise, then Christ is not risen.*

"And if Christ is not risen, your faith is futile; you are still in your sins! *Then also those who have fallen asleep in Christ have perished. If in this life only we have hope in Christ, we are of all men the most pitiable"* (1 Corinthians 15:12-19).

A miracle is a special act of God that interrupts the natural course of events. One of the greatest miracles of all time is Christ's resurrection from the dead. Many times we focus our attention on the cross of Christ instead of the resurrection of

Christ. But there is nothing miraculous about dying on a cross. Anyone can die on a cross and many have. However, only one person in all of history has predicted and accomplished His own resurrection from the dead.

Consider this quote:

> "Indeed, since the credibility of Christianity rests on the resurrection of Christ (1 Corinthians 15:12–19), the whole of the orthodox Christian faith crumbles if miracles do not occur. If historic biblical Christianity is to survive and make sense to the modern mind, it is necessary to provide a reasonable explanation of the supernatural. Apart from the credibility of the biblical account of miracles, we can bid farewell to orthodox Christianity. Such is the challenge before us."[29]

Miracles are critical to Christianity and the greatest miracle has already happened: Creation. In the beginning, God **CREATED** (Genesis 1:1). You cannot disprove miracles without disproving God. "If we admit God, must we then admit miracles? Indeed, indeed, you have no security against it."[30] The Christian concept of the miraculous immediately depends on the existence of a theistic God. In order to defend the truth about miracles, we must first prove there is a God.

Just to review, we can know God exists. The **Cosmological Argument** says that anything that has a beginning has a beginner. The universe had a beginning and must have a Beginner. The **Teleological Argument** states that anything that has a design has a designer. Design can be seen in the biggest and smallest things in creation. The universe has a designer. The **Moral Argument**

---

[29] Norman L. Geisler, *Miracles and the Modern Mind: A Defense of Biblical Miracles* (Grand Rapids: Baker Book House, 1992), 10.

[30] C. S. Lewis, *Miracles, a Preliminary Study*, Macmillan Paperbacks Edition (New York: Macmillan, 1947), 169.

says if there is a moral law then there is a moral lawgiver. Since there are morally good and bad things in this world, there must be a moral gauge or law by which we decide. If there is a moral law then there must be a moral lawgiver.

MIRACLES OF THE BIBLE

Miracles in the Bible fall into three clusters based on the period of time when they occurred. The clusters are the mosaic (Moses), prophetic (Elijah/Elisha), and apostolic periods (Christ/ Apostles). First, each of these clusters of miracles marks a transition when God is **doing** something new. Second, they mark new revelation when God is **saying** something new. Last, they mark a new confirmation where God is **confirming someone** new.

A true miracle is always immediate, always successful, always lasts, and always glorifies God. Three purposes of miracles are to glorify God, to accredit certain people to speak for Him, and to provide evidence for belief in Him. Further, miracles take on the character of God and mirror the three arguments for God mentioned in Chapter 2. Miracles have an instantaneous beginning (Cosmological Argument), design and purpose (Teleological Argument), and promote good (Moral Argument).

EVENTS NOT STORIES

In order to defend our faith, we must be able to prove that miracles are both possible and actual. When we teach the Bible, we do well to emphasize that we are dealing with historic **EVENTS** and not just **STORIES**. This is especially true when dealing with children. Helping kids clearly see the difference between the facts of the Bible and the fiction they see in entertainment is critical to their understanding of faith in Christ.

Norman Geisler wrote the following about how miracles are viewed by unbelievers:

"The Bible is laced with miracles. From the Creation to the Second Coming, from Moses at the burning bush, to Daniel in the lions' den, from the Virgin Birth to the Resurrection, miraculous happenings seem to fill the pages of Scripture. To the believer, these are a wonderful confirmation of the power and message of God, but to the unbeliever, miracles are a stumbling block—a proof that religion is just a bunch of fairy tales after all. In the world that he lives in, there is no divine intervention, no interruptions to the normal order; there is only natural law. Fire consumes when it burns; lions eat whatever is available; pregnancy only happens when male sperm unite with female ova, and the dead stay dead. As far as they are concerned, the miracles of the Bible could no more be true than Mother Goose."[31]

Some in the Bible did not believe in Jesus even when they came face to face with a miraculous event. John grieved, *"Even after Jesus had performed so many signs in their presence, they still would not believe in Him"* (John 12:37, NIV). Jesus Himself said of some, *"They will not be convinced even if someone rises from the dead"* (Luke 16:31, NIV).

MIRACLES TODAY?

There is no need to fight too hard to prove that miracles happen. Instead, first prove that God exists and miracles naturally follow. However, there is true confusion about things that happen today that might be called miracles.

Is it possible that some miracles and signs are no longer active? If a person goes to the doctor and is diagnosed with cancer and is later found to be cancer free, is that a miracle? The word

---

[31] Norman L. Geisler and Ronald M. Brooks, *When Skeptics Ask* (Wheaton: Victor Books, 1990), 75.

"miracle" is used so casually today that the power of the biblical miracles lose their credibility. The miracles found in the Bible should be held in high regard. Perhaps we should reserve a special category for them that is separate from things that happen today that are called "miracles".

I would like to suggest using a capital "M" when dealing with the **M**iracles found in the Bible. I do this as an act of personal discipline in order to emphasize the special role biblical Miracles played in the time they happened and continue to hold for readers today. It is clear that miracles still happen today. However, the miracles that happen today do not serve the same purposes as the **M**iracles in the Bible. Further, there are at least five other categories of unusual things that we experience and hear about today that are not miracles. See the chart below.

THERE ARE AT LEAST SIX DIFFERENT CATEGORIES OF UNUSUAL EVENTS:						
	ANOMALIES	MAGIC	PSYCHOSOMATIC	SATANIC SIGNS	PROVIDENCE	MIRACLES
DESCRIPTION	Freaks of nature	Sleight of hand	Mind over matter	Evil power	Prearranged events	Divine act
POWER	Physical	Human	Mental	Psychic	Divine	Supernatural
TRAITS	Natural event with pattern	Unnatural and man-controlled	Requires faith; fails for some sickness	Evil, falsehood, occult, limited	Naturally explained; spiritual context	Never fails, immediate, lasts, glory to God
EXAMPLE	Bumblebee	Rabbit in hat	Psychosomatic cures	Demonic influence	Fog at Normandy	Raising the dead

GOD'S PROVIDENCE

People today, especially Christians, use the term "miracle" rather loosely. Many times, an event is labeled a miracle when it should be more accurately described as God's providence. God causes providential events indirectly, but not directly. He uses natural laws to accomplish them instead of interrupting the natural course of events.

The fog at Normandy concealed the attack against the evil Nazi army. Although God may have been behind it, the fog was providential and not miraculous, because it can be explained by natural laws. A prayer that is answered, or some especially good thing that happens in your life, may be an example of God's providence and not necessarily a miracle. These events may stimulate your faith as they are **supernormal**, but they are not **supernatural**.

WHY PRAY?

Have you ever prayed for a miracle?

"And this is the confidence that we have toward Him, that if we ask anything according to His will He hears us. And if we know that He hears us in whatever we ask, we know that we have the requests that we have asked of Him" (1 John 5:14–15, ESV).

Because God is immutable or unchanging it is easy to wonder why we should pray. Is this passage saying that we can ask God for anything and He will miraculously give it to us? This seems unlikely based on the context. In this passage, obedience to God's commands and a willingness to serve God by doing "what pleases Him" are conditions for receiving. In Chapter 5 of 1 John, John also adds that what we ask for should be in line with His will.

In order to enjoy the **power** of prayer, we must understand the **purpose** of prayer. God is not a genie in a bottle. He is an all-knowing, all-powerful, all-good Being who desires to pour out **HIS BLESSINGS** on His people. Prayer is not our way of getting our will done in Heaven. It is God's way of getting His will done on Earth. *"God is not man, that he should lie, nor a son of man, that he should change his mind"* (Numbers 23:19, ESV). Prayer doesn't change God, but it changes things. God is the unchanging Changer of all things. He is the unmoving Mover of all things.

Consider this illustration by Dr. Tony Evans. "If I put a million dollars in your physical bank account, you are a guaranteed millionaire. But if you don't know how to write a check, that which is guaranteed cannot be enjoyed. Too many of us who've got bank accounts full of God's blessing are forgetting to sign our checks. We forget to draw from that spiritual reservoir, or we don't understand how to draw from that spiritual reservoir to live the successful Christian life."

Prayer is not our way of getting our will done in Heaven. It is God's way of getting His will done on Earth.

PART TWO:

THE BIG CONTENDERS

PROVE IT

CHAPTER 4

THE TRUTH ABOUT WORLD RELIGIONS

The second section of *Prove It* covers the "Big Contenders" to the Christian faith—world religions and cults. This second section is transitional and connects the first and last sections. The goal is for you to know as much information as possible about the "Big Contenders" before moving into the "Big Criticism" section of this book. With this knowledge, the various failed attempts by cults and other world religions to deal with the problem of evil will be easily identified and understood.

WORLD RELIGIONS

The world is full of religious people. At first glance, this simple statement has the potential to comfort someone who is concerned for the spiritual well-being of people. However, this would be a false sense of comfort. Because of the wide variety of religious groups, there are many who are teaching false doctrines and pointing people to a false sense of truth.

More than ever, there is a great need for evangelical Christians to understand, and act on, the truth about God. "Christians who seek to be relevant to the world in which they live must understand the beliefs of the people with whom they share the globe."[32] Further, this is not just a situation that exists abroad or that should be considered only by mission-minded people of faith. "Almost everyone living on this planet today must cope with the presence of differing beliefs and forms of worship right in their own backyards."[33]

Resistant to Definition

One challenge that surfaces when discussing the topic of world religions is the task of adequately defining the word *religion*. In many ways, it is a term that resists definition. Even when a meaning can be agreed upon, it is many times still somewhat subjective. For the purpose of this book, *religion* is defined as "a system of beliefs and practices that provides values to give life meaning and coherence by directing a person toward transcendence."[34]

A world religion differs from a cult in that a cult is usually a deviation from a specific world religion. Unlike a cult, a world religion has an origin completely independent of any other religion and commonly teaches that other world religions are inferior and wrong. Generally speaking, most world religions have a global reach as well as some type of unique ritualistic aspect.

The Chicken or the Egg?

Which came first, religion or man? More specifically, did religion begin with humans or with God? In Acts 17, Paul encounters the men of Athens and finds that they are very religious:

"Then Paul stood in the midst of the Areopagus and said, "Men of Athens, I perceive that in all things you are very religious; for as I was passing through and considering the objects of your worship, I

---

[32] Winfried Corduan, *Neighboring Faiths: A Christian Introduction to World Religions* (Downers Grove: InterVarsity Press, 1998), 14.
[33] Ibid., 13.
[34] Corduan, 21.

even found an altar with this inscription: TO THE UNKNOWN GOD. Therefore, the One whom you worship without knowing, Him I proclaim to you: God, who made the world and everything in it, since He is Lord of heaven and earth, does not dwell in temples made with hands. Nor is He worshiped with men's hands, as though He needed anything, since He gives to all life, breath, and all things" (Acts 17:22-25).

In this passage, we see that the men of Athens are very involved with religious acts and Paul is careful to observe this and encourage them. However, Paul realizes that their activities are focused on false gods. It is of special interest to him that they have created an altar for the "in case of" god. Just in case they missed a god, they had an extra altar for any potential god they had not discovered yet. Paul uses that as a launching pad to teach them about the one true God.

However, what is the source of the intense religious activity that Paul observed? "Logically, there are four possible answers to the question of source. Religions find their source in humans, God, Satan, or some combination of these three."[35] Knowing that throughout all of history man has participated in religious activities, it would be simple to infer that humans are the source of religion. Simply put, "we find religion wherever we find humanity."[36] However, the Scriptures point out that God is the source of true religion and that all false religions flow from either man or Satan. The following verses highlight God as the ultimate source of all true religion:

"And God spoke all these words, saying: "I am the LORD your God, who brought you out of the land of Egypt, out of the house of bondage. You shall have no other gods before Me" (Exodus 20:1–3).

---

[35] Dockery, 880.
[36] Corduan, 22.

"Therefore know that the LORD your God, He is God, the faithful God who keeps covenant and mercy for a thousand generations with those who love Him and keep His commandments; and He repays those who hate Him to their face, to destroy them. He will not be slack with him who hates Him; He will repay him to his face. Therefore you shall keep the commandment, the statutes, and the judgments which I command you today, to observe them" (Deuteronomy 7:9–11).

"For since the creation of the world His invisible attributes are clearly seen, being understood by the things that are made, even His eternal power and Godhead, so that they are without excuse, because, although they knew God, they did not glorify Him as God, nor were thankful, but became futile in their thoughts, and their foolish hearts were darkened" (Romans 1:20–21).

Both the Old and New Testaments teach that God is the source of true religion. It follows that when it comes to false religions, we should see "religion as an intrinsically human phenomenon rather than the product of an encounter with an external reality."[37]

The World of Religions

A broad look at the situation with respect to all active world religions causes great concern for those who are to defend the Christian faith. In 2006, the world population was 6,500,000,000. Of that, 2,156,000,000 (33%) of the world were professing Christians. Another 4,344,000,000 (67%) were non-Christians, and of that percentage, 3,419,000,000 (53%) were religious non-Christians.[38] In other words, over half of the world's population in 2006 was actively religious, but not actually Christian.

---

[37] Ibid.

[38] Marsha A. Ellis Smith., *Holman Book of Biblical Charts, Maps, and Reconstructions* (Nashville: Broadman and Holman Publishers, 1993), 28.

This means that half of the world is involved in religious activity without any connection to the One who is actually worthy of worship. Knowing that over half of the religious people in the world are not Christian should be a call to action for those who are concerned with the spiritual well-being of people around the world. Because of the wide variety of religious groups, many that teach false doctrines and point people to a false sense of truth, there is a great need for evangelical Christians to understand, and act on, the truth about God.

Different Roots

Christianity is founded in the God of the Bible and holds that the Bible is wholly true in all that it affirms. There are no errors or contradictions in the Bible and God speaks primarily through His Word. As taught in the Bible, Christianity is rooted in Jesus Christ, who alone is the source of life. Jesus is fully God and fully man and is thus the "God-man."

Jesus lived a perfect life and is the Son of God. Because of His death on the cross, sin is no longer the issue between man and God (John 3:16). It is because of His perfect sacrifice on our behalf that we are freed from the penalty of sin. Jesus claimed to be exclusively the way, the truth, and the life, and said that no one comes to the Father except though Him (John 14:6). By grace alone, through faith alone (Ephesians 2:8-9), in Christ alone, a person can move from a place of death and separation from God to a place of everlasting life and fellowship with God.

Different Results

The final results of Christianity are also an important difference to understand, as there is great variety in the beliefs of different world religions. Specifically, there are many ideas as to how a fully developed "religious" person should look and act in each of the main world religions. Once a person has believed in Jesus Christ for eternal life, he looks forward to a life lived free from the power of sin and an eternity experienced free from the very presence of sin.

In Christianity, a fully developed believer will have the character of Christ in their life as they learn to die to themselves (Luke 9:23-24), so that the character of Christ can be uninhibitedly expressed in them. As a result, another attribute of the developing Christian is the Fruit of the Spirit, which Paul outlines to the Galatians:

"But the fruit of the Spirit is love, joy, peace, forbearance, kindness, goodness, faithfulness, gentleness, and self-control. Against such things there is no law. Those who belong to Christ Jesus have crucified the flesh with its passions and desires. Since we live by the Spirit, let us keep in step with the Spirit. Let us not become conceited, provoking and envying each other" (Galatians 5:22-26, NIV).

The afterlife should also be a point of discussion with someone who has been previously involved in a world religion other than Christianity. A former Hindu, for example, should be exposed to the Christian belief of what happens after death because the two religions differ drastically on this subject.

Different Doctrine

The most important doctrinal differences to correctly understand are those concerning God and man. Because each world religion has a different view on who God is, or who the gods are, it will be necessary to clearly describe the God of the Bible. It cannot be overemphasized that preconceived ideas planted in the potential convert's mind by another world religion must be wiped away and replaced by an accurate teaching about God.

Once there is a clear understanding of God, it will be possible to understand more about humanity in relation to God's character and attributes. Christianity holds that God is one. However, there are three persons in God: the Father, the Son, and the Holy Spirit. As confusing as this is for many Christians, it is even more of a challenge for an individual who has been involved with another world religion.

The fact that God is one *What* with three *Whos* is foreign to a Muslim or a Hindu. For the Muslim, there is only one god, Allah, so the Trinity is offensive. For the Hindu, there is an endless supply of gods, so the Trinity seems limited. This is one of the challenges that a Hindu may have with a Christian who is attempting to evangelize him. "If you are already worshiping 330 million gods, it requires no particularly big effort to add one more to the group. 'Recognize Christ as Savior and invite him into your heart? Why not? It can't hurt.'"[39]

The issue with this thinking is that Christ's claims to be God are exclusive, and Christianity does not allow for any other God. Perhaps, the best illustration for the Trinity of God is a triangle as seen below:

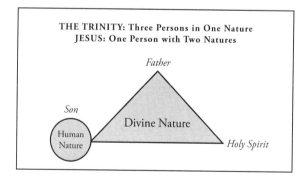

<hr>

[39] Corduan, 216-217.

Although this is a difficult concept to fully understand, it is a foundational doctrine of the Christian church. There are a number of analogies that may help the new Christian understand this better, but the triangle above is probably the most appropriate. Jesus, in His humanity (the circle), is an expression that is connected with His deity (the triangle) but cannot overlap. If the humanity of Christ and the Deity of Christ were to overlap in this illustration, then the infinite and finite would overlap, which logically cannot happen.

Well-known pastor and author Tony Evans points out that, "If you believe that Texas has a capital and I believe that Texas has a capital, it sounds like we believe the same thing. However, if one person thinks the capital is Fort Worth, and someone else thinks the capital is Austin, they do not believe the same thing. Believing in one capital doesn't mean we believe in the same thing."[40] Once there is a firm understanding of who God is and what God does, an understanding of man and his condition can be achieved.

Case Study: Hinduism and Buddhism

Hinduism is the third-largest world religion, consisting of 13.9% of the world's population. Buddhists make up 6%. Combining these percentages would move these two world religions into second place behind Christianity. Hinduism is the primary religion of India. "The name itself, actually a label devised by Westerners, simply means 'the religion of India.'"[41]

There are three main parts to the religion of Hinduism: the way of works, the way of knowledge, and the way of devotion.

---

[40] Tony Evans, *Tony Evans' Book of Illustrations: Stories, Quotes, and Anecdotes from More Than 30 Years of Preaching and Public Speaking* (Chicago: Moody Publishers, 2009), 330.

[41] Corduan, 216-217.

When dealing with a Hindu, it is important to keep in mind that "Hinduism prides itself on its tolerant attitude toward all world religions."[42] This allows Hindus to consider Christianity a legitimate way to find fulfillment in God but not the only way to find salvation in God.

The understanding of God and man, as well as how they relate to each other, is a crucial difference that a new Christian coming from Hinduism needs to understand. "Why should not the Christian simply hold up the gospel as one option for the Hindu to explore if he or she finds a lack of fulfillment in Hinduism? Why do Christians have to insist that theirs is the only way to fulfillment? The answer is that Christianity is not about fulfillment but about salvation from sin and its effects."[43]

Christians often mistakenly assume that Buddhists worship Buddha in a similar way to how Christians worship the God of the Bible. However, "It is important to realize that the Buddha is not crucial to the essence of Buddhism. He is the teacher and the initiator, and he is venerated by millions of Buddhists. But millions of other Buddhists worship different Buddhas and spiritual beings; still others say that worship of any being has no place in Buddhism."[44]

When talking with a person who has been influenced by Buddhism, it is important to know that there are a large number of differing beliefs and rituals within Buddhism. Another point of interest is that the roots of Buddhism are grounded in a history of religious speculations. In contrast, Christianity is rooted in historically accurate **events,** not speculative **stories**. As with many of the cults, Buddhists lack any eyewitness accounts of the stories that are foundational to their religion.

---

[42] Ibid., 216.
[43] Ibid., 217.
[44] Ibid., 220.

The Apostle Peter speaks of this important distinction: *"For we did not follow cunningly devised fables when we made known to you the power and coming of our Lord Jesus Christ, but were eyewitnesses of His majesty"* (2 Peter 1:16). Because of this distinction, as well the lack of a clear answer as to what a person must do to be saved, former Buddhists should find great comfort in the strong foundations of the Christian faith. This is because the result of the work of Jesus Christ in a believer's life is full redemption and relationship with God.

Case Study: Islam

Islam is the second largest religion in the world with more than 18% of the world's population claiming to be Muslim. Islam is found not only in the Middle East but also throughout Asia, Africa, Europe, and North America. There are many doctrines of Islam that are, at best, confusing, because they are self-contradictory. The highest authority in the religion of Islam is the Quran, which teaches that there is only one god, Allah. Muhammad, who was supposedly visited by the Angel Gabriel in A.D. 610 on what is now known as the Mount of Light, founded Islam.

Muhammad is not the only Islamic prophet. Many of the prophets of Islam are actually biblical figures, including Adam, Noah, Abraham, David, and Jesus. Muhammed also acknowledged Jesus as being a great prophet, but rejected the idea that Jesus was God and that He actually died on the cross. This is obviously in direct conflict with the words of Christ and is one of the many contradictions between Islam and Christianity.

If Moses and Jesus were prophets from God, why are there discrepancies between the Bible and the Quran with regard to their lives and teachings? The traditional Islamic answer is that all the prophets taught the message that Muhammad taught. But subsequently people tampered with the writings they left behind and distorted the truth of the original message. As one drastic example, Muslims say that Christ did not claim to be God. Passages in which He apparently did so (for example, John 10:30) they claim to be later fabrications by the Christian church.[45]

When an individual with previous exposure to Islam is faced with these contradictions, it may be difficult to relate to other Christians. His previous experiences will cause Him to struggle with the Trinity of God as well as the inerrancy of the Bible. In addition, although he may have believed in Christ, there may still be confusion about Christ's deity. Many Muslims disregard Christianity for these reasons, arguing that these claims are absurd. Islam makes more sense to them because it is simple.

From Religion to Relationship

In order to embrace the truth, individuals with a background in other world religions need to experience the power of a relationship with Jesus Christ. Religious activity will not be enough to satisfy. Only through knowing and growing in Jesus Christ can Christian maturity be completed (Colossians 2:10). The Scripture commands that we are to "press on" in order to "lay hold" of Christ (Philippians 3:12).

In order to find spiritual wholeness in Christ, we must better know who Christ is, and the only way to do that is by spending time in communication with Him. Through the disciplines of prayer and Bible study, communication with God can become rich and rewarding. An environment of grace and not legalism is important. One of the consistent and sustained teachings of Paul throughout the NT is that salvation comes by grace alone, through faith alone, in Christ alone (Ephesians 2:8-9).

However, other world religions, and even many Christian

---

[45] Ibid., 78.

organizations, will deny this and teach their followers that they must work for their salvation. It is important to distinguish between justification salvation (being saved from the penalty of sin), sanctification salvation (being saved from the power of sin), and glorification salvation (being saved from the presence of sin). Specifically, it is sanctification that is of utmost importance for the new convert that is seeking spiritual wholeness.

CHAPTER 5

THE TRUTH ABOUT CULTS

CULT IN OUR CULTURE

Regarding cults, it is important to state what is, perhaps, obvious. There is a problem. The problem is one that the evangelical church has allowed to develop and has, unfortunately, inadequately addressed. Because of a lack of genuine and persuasive Bible teaching, passionate evangelism, and sustained discipleship, cults are in our culture.

In many ways, as one author put it, the cults are "the unpaid bills of the church."[46] The New Testament church has a clear mandate to spread the truth, and also defend it, because "a man who will not stand for something will quite likely fall for almost anything."[47] The sad devotion to nothing at all is exactly what we are increasingly seeing in our communities. Individuals who have not convincingly been engaged by the truths of the Bible are now a large part of both our communities, and sadly, our churches.

---

[46] Jan Karel Van Baalen, *The Chaos of Cults: A Study of Present-day Isms*, 4th Revelation (Grand Rapids: Eerdmans Pub., 1962), 14.

[47] Walter Martin, *The Kingdom of the Cults*, Revelation (Minneapolis: Bethany House Publishers, 2003), 18.

"The only 'faith' not acceptable in our liberal churches today is biblical faith that dares to make exclusive claims about Jesus Christ, the gospel, the Bible, and salvation!"[48] Jehovah's Witnesses, Mormons, and many other deviations from evangelical Christianity are growing in both number and impact. Leading apologists Norman Geisler and Ron Rhodes report that "some experts say there are about 700 cults, while others say there are as many as 3,000. Cults of one form or another involve more than 20 million people in the United States, and they are multiplying at an alarming rate."[49]

One trend that has fueled the growth of the cults in our culture is the increase in relativistic thinking in our society. Truth is no longer accepted as being objective but rather subjective. This type of subjective thinking leaves the words of the Bible, and those who teach them, powerless, unless they are met by an audience which at least affirms absolute truth. "The nature of truth is crucial to the Christian faith. Not only does Christianity claim there is absolute truth (truth for everyone, everywhere, at all times), but it insists that truth about the world (reality) is that which corresponds to the way things really are."[50] As objective truth is attacked, an increased emphasis on the individual and his personal feelings grows and allows for moral rebellion and a customized belief system to accommodate the lifestyle desired by the individual.

What is a Cult?

The word *cult* is an interesting word to attempt to define because the word itself has a subjective nature. Because a cult is

---

[48] Ibid., 21.
[49] Norman L. Geisler and Ron Rhodes, *When Cultists Ask: A Popular Handbook on Cultic Misinterpretations,* elect. (Grand Rapids: Baker Books, 1997).
[50] Norman L. Geisler, *Baker Encyclopedia of Christian Apologetics*, Baker Reference Library (Grand Rapids: Baker Books, 1999), 741.

defined as a deviation from a particular religion, it is necessary to know the religion in question before developing a useful definition. Arriving at the appropriate meaning of the word is even more challenging as it depends on the context. In addition, it is possible to be "cultish" without actually being a cult. Therefore, we must not confuse the activities of a cult with the teachings of a cult. However, it should be said that the word *cult* is, by nature, a derogatory word with a negative connotation. "There is no universally agreed-upon definition of a cult; there are only some generally recognizable traits. Actually, there are three different dimensions of a cult—doctrinal, sociological, and moral."[51]

For the purpose of this book, a cult will be defined as any false religious teaching, other than another world religion, that goes against the doctrines of the Christian faith. Cults are also known for their deceptive and aggressive witnessing practices. The Mormons have an unusually aggressive approach to sharing their beliefs. "Even surpassing the Jehovah's Witnesses is the rapidly burgeoning missionary effort of the church of Jesus Christ of Latter-day Saints (Mormon)."[52]

It is not just at the front doors of homes that the cults are making strides to reach the world with a message of confusion. "When it is pointed out that in 1997, less than half of the membership of Jehovah's Witnesses resides in the United States, the gravity of the problem that confronts the Christian church is apparent to all but the most adamantly obtuse."[53] Cults are a serious and growing concern all over the world as they are an aggressive challenge to evangelical Christianity. Now, more than ever, the church needs to be ready with an answer and a defense for the hope that is in us (1 Peter 3:15).

---

[51] Geisler and Rhodes.
[52] Martin, 427.
[53] Ibid., 425.

Arguably, the most important need is to make sure that new and/or young Christians are exposed to proper discipleship and equipped to stand firm in the truth. The Word of God teaches clearly that it is God's will that all men come to the saving knowledge of His son Jesus Christ (1 Timothy 2:4). Our God waits patiently, not desiring that anyone perish (2 Peter 3:9). As God's chosen people, it is our responsibility to reach out to those who are in cults, with the message of God's grace through His Son, Jesus Christ, knowing that they can be won over by the truth.

Reaching the Cultist

In order to individually and corporately reach out to those who are lost in cults, there are some biblical characteristics that we should adopt in order to be effective. First, is a love that puts the cultist before even ourselves (1 Corinthians 13:5-7). Without this attitude of love, a sacrificial love, it will be very easy for one to get distracted while attempting to reach out to those who have been deceived and lied to by the cults. Second, is a commitment to the discipleship process (Ephesians 5:1-7) and a sustained investment in the individual. Without effective discipleship, there is no way for any individual to grow in the knowledge of Jesus Christ.

Third, it would be valuable for these individuals to receive clear teachings about the cults they came from as well as others. Most importantly, he should be instructed about the one true God (2 Timothy 2:24-26). Finally, there should be a commitment to prayer, for and by the cultist. The Bible teaches that if anyone has trouble, that he should pray (James 5:13). This is certainly true in the life of a new convert that is working out the truth in the local church. The book of James offers one other important teaching regarding a brother in Christ who wanders from the truth:

"Brethren, if anyone among you wanders from the truth, and someone turns him back, let him know that he who turns a sinner from the error of his way will save a soul from death and cover a multitude of sins" (James 5:19-20).

Even after a person has become part of the church they can still turn away, get distracted, and become entangled in a lie or sin. Despite having a true understanding of who Jesus Christ is and that salvation comes by grace alone, through faith alone, in Christ alone, it is still possible for that person to wander from the truth. In circumstances like this, fellow believers are charged with the responsibility to reach out and work diligently to turn the brother or sister away from their error.

Perhaps the most disheartening aspect of dealing with someone who is entangled in a cult is realizing that, no matter what you say, some will still resist the truth. Some people do not want to know that they are wrong. It is easier to keep going on the path they have started than to try to make a change.

Definite on Doctrine

Cult doctrine is what the Bible refers to as false teaching. Many New Testament writers wrote about false teaching and documented what Jesus taught regarding false teachers and prophets. Jesus warned that false teachers would come and deceive many people (Matthew 24:5). He also warned that false prophets will be easy to follow because they will come in sheep's clothing but inwardly are ravenous wolves (Matthew 7:15-23). "Since the earliest days of Christianity, both the apostle and disciple alike have been confronted with the perversion of the revelation God has given us in the person of Jesus Christ."[54]

John also warned his readers of those who would deny Jesus Christ and would not have the truth in them (1 John 2:19-22).

---

[54] Ibid., 434.

The apostle Paul taught of his desire to continue teaching because of the false teachers that would come (2 Corinthians 11:12-15).

Paul went further by charging the church in Rome to "abhor what is evil" and to love what is good (Romans 12:9). Although many cults actually accept the Bible as "a" source of truth, the cultist must be encouraged to accept the Bible as the highest authority of truth. As a part of this thinking, he must begin to explore new ground and realize he has immediate access to the truth through God's Word.

Most cults have deviated from the Christian faith, not necessarily in practice but in doctrine, and will deny one or more of the tenets of the historic Christian faith. Cultists commonly affirm extra-biblical sources of authority and often claim to be the only true and pure form of Christianity. Two main areas of doctrine that are attacked by cults are justification by faith alone and the deity of Jesus Christ.

As these concepts are being dealt with, it is important to note that many cultists will still struggle to accept what they are hearing. "According to the Watchtower … the clergy of Christendom are obviously the villains and are the objects of 'pure hatred' … clergymen are therefore always suspect and their theology is to be regarded as untrustworthy and inspired by Satan."[55] If the former cultist does not know what authentic Biblical teaching is, he will always be vulnerable to false teaching. The following illustrates this idea:

"The American Banking Association has a training program that exemplifies the aim of the author. Each year it sends hundreds of bank tellers to Washington in order to teach them to detect counterfeit money, which is a great source of a loss of revenue to the Treasury Department. It is most interesting that during the

---

[55] Martin, 44.

entire two-week training program, no teller touches counterfeit money. The reason for this is that the American Banking Association is convinced that if a man is thoroughly familiar with the original, he will not be deceived by the counterfeit bill, no matter how much like the original it appears. It is the contention of this writer that if the average Christian would become familiar once again with the great foundations of his faith, he would be able to detect those counterfeit elements so apparent in the cult systems, which set apart from biblical Christianity."[56]

Definite on Jesus Christ

Jesus Christ was more than a great man and prophet, He was and is God. Jesus lived a perfect life on earth and was fully God and fully man. Many cultists argue against this, saying that Jesus was God's Son but not God. Their rationale is that being God's Son somehow means that Jesus could not be God. However, Jesus being God's Son does not disqualify Him from being deity. If anything, it supports the argument for Jesus that He is divine. If a human has a child, although the child is the son or daughter of the parent, the child is still human. The relationship between the parent and the child does not prove that the child is not human. On the contrary, it confirms the humanity of the child.

In the same way, the relationship between Jesus the Son and God the Father does not prove that Jesus is not deity. However, this is what many of the cults will teach. The Jehovah's Witnesses' New World Translation actually renders John 1:1, "The Word was a god" in an attempt to resolve their belief that Jesus Christ was the Son of God, a good prophet, a perfect man, but not God. "It's not psychology, it's not sociology, it's not anthropology, it's Christology, what you believe about Jesus Christ, which makes

---

[56] Ibid., 23.

the difference for eternity."[57]

It is also important to understand Jesus' role as the mediator between God and man. The Bible describes Jesus as the mediator (1 Timothy 2:5-6). Cults, specifically Jehovah's Witnesses, will use this passage to argue that Jesus cannot be God because He is the mediator. The problem with this argument is that Jesus could not be man either. If Jesus is disqualified from being God because He is the mediator between God and man, then He must also be disqualified from being man for the exact same reason. However, most cults believe that Jesus was indeed a man.

Another struggle of the false teaching of cults is the idea that Jesus is not God, because, it is argued, Jesus was actually created, and is therefore part of creation, rather than being uncreated. The Bible teaches that Jesus is the firstborn of creation (Colossians 1:15), and this is twisted to mean that Jesus is actually part of creation. However, this is not what this passage is saying. Paul wrote this passage to affirm Christ's preeminence over all creation, not His place in creation. Christ is firstborn in the sense that He is first in rank in God's kingdom. This passage also teaches that Jesus created all things (Colossians 1:16), which brings up an interesting conflict if He is also a creature.

This is one of the discussions that visiting Mormons will often bring to the table when they visit a home. Their argument is that Jesus was not God because Colossians 1:15 shows that He is a creature. However, when asked about Jesus' role in the creation process, they quickly affirm that He was part of it. In fact, they will actually argue that Jesus created everything for God. However, this begs the question, how could Jesus be both the Creator of all things and a creature?

---

[57] Ibid., 59.

If there is only one Creator and if Jesus is not God, whom they agree is the Creator; there are now two Creators, Jesus and God. Clear thinking can resolve this, but "if cultists don't think, then thinking can't be the key to mental liberation."[58] Jesus clearly claimed to be God and often acted the part. However, He did not just claim it or act it, He proved it. He did so with three unparalleled proofs:

1. He fulfilled numerous messianic prophecies written hundreds of years in advance.

2. He lived a sinless life and performed miraculous deeds.

3. He predicted and then accomplished his own resurrection from the dead.[59]

Definite on Justification

When the New Testament is properly studied and taught, there is absolutely no other conclusion than that salvation comes through faith alone and not by works. In addition, when "Christianity denies the biblical faith it ceases to be Christianity at all."[60] One of the consistent and sustained teachings of Paul throughout the New Testament is that salvation comes by grace alone, through faith alone, in Christ alone (Ephesians 2:8-9). However, cults will deny this and teach their followers that they must work for their salvation.

It is important to distinguish between justification salvation (being saved from the penalty of sin), sanctification salvation (being saved from the power of sin), and glorification salvation (being saved from the presence of sin). Specifically, it is justification that is the source of much debate by a cultist. Although many

---

[58] Ibid., 72.
[59] Geisler and Turek, 347.
[60] Martin, 21.

cults teach that a person can lose their salvation, this is in direct conflict with the teachings of the Bible. Jesus said that His sheep hear His voice and they follow Him, and no one can snatch them out of His hand (John 10:28). Because Jesus offers life that is everlasting (John 3:16), there is no end to the salvation believers experience in Him.

The strength of a person's faith is not what saves him; it is the object of that person's faith that makes an eternal difference in his life. When one places his faith in a cult's counterfeit christ, it makes no difference how many good works he does as a part of his religious journey. He will still be condemned. However, if a person places his faith in the God-Man Jesus Christ that is presented in the Bible, it makes no difference how many terrible things he has done. That person's belief will result in everlasting life.

Further, the life of obedience must be understood as an outflow of the faith an individual already has. Instead, many cults teach that being obedient and doing good works are the way a person can ultimately, one day, earn salvation. Simply put, the emphasis must be shifted from religion to relationship.

Studying The Bible

Effective Bible study is one of the most important aspects to understanding and dealing with cults. The Bible is not just another religious book. It is God's primary vehicle for communicating His truth to the contemporary world. Without a commitment to getting in the Word, and letting the Word get in you, it will be very easy for an individual who is attempting to defend Christianity to fall short of being able to make a real impact. Only the power and truth of God's Word will be able to make a lasting and sustained impact in life. Because of this, it is vital that Christian apologists get involved in effective Bible study.

Longtime Christian educator and seminary professor How-ard Hendricks presents a three-step process of Bible study in his book, *Living by the Book*.[61] Because of the centrality of the Bible to the Christian apologetics, the skill of effective Bible study must be cultivated. The three-step process that Hendricks out-lines includes Observation, Interpretation, and Application.

Observation is the first step. "In this step, you ask and an-swer the question, *What do I see?* The moment you come to the Scriptures you ask, what are the facts? You assume the role of the biblical detective, looking for clues. No detail is trivial."[62] In this step, the student of the Bible will look at terms, objects, people, actions, etc., in the passage that is being studied. The goal here is to hold back from making any interpretations of the passage until the student knows as much as possible about what is in the passage.

The second step is **interpretation**. "Here you ask and answer the question, *What does it mean?* Your quest is for meaning. Un-fortunately, too much Bible study begins with interpretation, and furthermore, it usually ends there. However, I am going to show that it does not begin there. Before you understand, you have to learn to see."[63] Interpreting the Bible is a task that can cause much controversy in the church if there are two differing interpretations of the same passage. In this situation, how does one know which is right? Because there can be only one correct interpretation of any given passage, when there are differences, either one is right and the other is wrong, or they both are wrong. They cannot be in contradiction with each other and both be right. In addition, the Bible can never mean something today

---

[61] Howard G. Hendricks and William D. Hendricks, *Living by the Book* (Chicago: Moody Press, 1991).
[62] Ibid., 35.
[63] Ibid.

that it did not mean to its original audience. This means that the serious student of the Bible must also learn as much as possible about the original recipients of each passage in the Bible in order to accurately understand the meaning of that passage. Although there can be only one interpretation, there can be many applications of the truths found in the Bible.

The final step is **application**. "Here you ask and answer the question, *How does it work?* Not, does it work? People say they're going to make the Bible 'relevant.' However, if the Bible is not already relevant, nothing anyone does will help. The Bible is relevant because it is revealed. It is always a return to reality. And those who read it and heed it, it changes their lives."[64] The point here is that Bible study must go beyond just academics and be put into action. Once the meaning (singular) of a passage is found, applications (plural) can be made into the life of the Christian that will move him closer to God and His will.

What would the church look like today if every one of its members knew how to study the Bible properly and committed to doing it regularly? "Even though the Bible remains one of the most sold books in the world, it is also one of the most neglected ones. The Barna Research Group of Glendale, California reports that in a typical week only 10 percent of Americans read their Bible every day."[65] Despite the fact that technology has put at our fingertips more ways to read the Bible and access various commentaries and Bible study helps, there seems to be a general deterioration of Biblical integrity. One survey found "that 82 percent of Americans believe that the Bible is either the literal or 'inspired' Word of God. More than half say they read the Bible at least monthly. Yet half couldn't name even one of the four Gospels, Matthew, Mark, Luke, and John. And fewer than half knew

---

[64] Ibid., 35-36.
[65] Ibid., 10.

who delivered the Sermon on the Mount."[66]

Complex and Simple Teachings

In order to have good hermeneutics, there are a few additional rules to follow. For example, when there are passages that are confusing and/or controversial, it is always a good rule to read those passages with a more clear passage in mind and interpret them in light of the more simple passages. In the same way, if a complex passage is found, it should always be read and studied in light of more simple passages. Some of the more prevalent deviations from authentic Christianity, as presented in the Bible, arise from breaking this simple rule of hermeneutics.

For example, James 2 is a passage that confuses many and is often a source of theological controversy. Because of this, it should be interpreted in light of clear teachings by Paul throughout his epistles. Mormons quote this passage as an example of the Bible teaching works-based salvation. This is because they have used the more complex and confusing passage to interpret other parts of the Bible instead of using more simple passages, such as Ephesians 2:8-9 or John 3:16, to better understand this passage in James.

Individual and Group Teachings

Another hermeneutic rule that is important to understand involves Biblical teachings addressed to individuals or small groups being interpreted in light of teachings addressed to large groups. Many times in the Bible, we see Jesus and His disciples addressing an individual or small group with a teaching that seems to contradict something taught elsewhere in the Bible.

For example, when Jesus encountered the rich, young ruler,

---

[66] Ibid.

He told him to sell everything he owned and to give to the poor in order to inherit eternal life (Mark 10:17-22). Because Jesus is speaking to an individual, it is important to realize that this is primarily a descriptive passage and not a prescriptive one. In other words, this teaching is directed specifically at the man who asked the question and should not necessarily be taught as normative for all Christians.

We know that the New Testament writers do not consistently teach that everyone needs to sell everything they own and give it to the poor. It is important to read this passage in light of teachings that have been addressed to large groups such as Jesus' teachings in the Sermon on the Mount and Paul's writings to the various churches. Keeping this simple rule in mind helps prevent inaccurate interpretations.

Context, Context, Context

So many times the Bible is misinterpreted simply because the text is taken out of context. "Every major cult is built on a violation of the principle of context. But a great deal of that sort of doctrinal error could be corrected by simply asking, 'Would you please read the previous verses or the ones that follow?'"[67] Context is important in Bible study because words by themselves have a range of definitions, and their meaning can change depending on the context of the sentence. Sentences have meaning in the context of the paragraph. Paragraphs have meaning in the context of a chapter. Chapters have meaning in the context of a book. Books have meaning in the context of the entire Bible. A text without context is a pretext.

Warning!

In cults, there is not only a general disregard for context,

---

[67] Ibid., 226.

there is also a frequent and intentional redefining of terms. "We might say that in the kingdom of the cults we are actually seeing a mosaic of abnormal conditioned behavior patterns that express themselves in a theological framework, utilizing Christian terms perverted by redefinition and represented as 'new insight,' when in truth they are only old errors with new faces."[68]

It is somewhat difficult to navigate the tangled web of semantics that the cults weave. Authentic Christianity shares many terms with these other groups, but the cults replace the traditional usage of these common terms. "So it is possible for a Jehovah's Witnesses, a Christian Scientist, or a Mormon, for example, to utilize the terminology of biblical Christianity with absolute freedom, having already redesigned these terms in a theological framework of his own making and to his own liking, but almost always at direct variance with the historically accepted meanings of the terms."[69]

Cults also tend to take advantage of the fact that most Christians do not have the ability to critically listen to the terms that are being used. As the cultist speaks, he uses a customized vocabulary that carries a different set of meanings and definitions from that of the evangelical Christian. Words like *salvation, Jesus*, and *grace* all take on a subtle different twist when the cultist uses them. "The careful Christian will thoughtfully and conscientiously learn the cult's unique vocabularies and properly represent that cult's beliefs in order to carry on a meaningful and significant dialogue with a cultist."[70]

Although this may sound like a simple task, it is often complicated by the ever so evasive tactics used by the cultist to avoid

---

[68] Martin, 48.
[69] Ibid.
[70] Ibid., 29.

precise definitions of the terms in question. It is important to understand that every term used goes through a filter of false teaching and is potentially heard in a completely different way than intended. The following chart has a few of the terms that are commonly redefined by cults.[71]

Cult	Term	Cult Definition	Christian Definition
Mormonism	God	Many gods	One God
Jehovah's Witnesses	Jesus Christ	Not god, created by Jehovah	God the Son, Creator of all
Christian Science	Sin	Illusion, error, not real	Disobedience to God
New Age	Salvation	Becoming One with the Universe/God	Reconciliation with God by means of Christ's atonement

---

[71] Ibid., 32.

PART THREE:

THE BIG CRITICISM

PROVE IT

CHAPTER 6

THE TRUTH ABOUT EVIL, PART 1

"WHY?"

Probably every one of us can think of a time when we cried out to God, "Why me?" Everyone experiences pain. It is the common ground on which all humanity stands. Every living person is in the process of pain management. The REAL question is WHY must it be this way? Why must we deal with pain and suffering? Why doesn't God help us? Why doesn't He heal the sick? Why doesn't He stop women from being raped? Why must people that we love die?

The final section of this book covers the problem of evil, pain, and suffering. This is a real-life issue of the **heart** for both believers and unbelievers. However, this is a problem that must be resolved with the **mind**.

The Problem of Evil

Throughout the years, theology has presented the thinking man with many difficult questions. Some are very specific to an individual's belief system while others cross over into every person's experience as a human. The problem of evil is an issue that touches every individual during the course of life.

No one is able to avoid the reality that life provides many opportunities for experiencing evil and pain firsthand. In fact, the problem of evil is considered "the most serious intellectual obstacle that stands between many people and religious faith."[72] The three major worldviews each have a unique response to evil. Pantheism affirms God and denies evil. Atheism affirms evil and denies God. Theism affirms both God and evil.

From a theistic worldview, a serious academic problem arises. From life's first cry, the human experience is one of pain for both the child and mother. In addition, death involves pain, often for the dying and always for the people who are left behind to grieve the loss of a loved one. Perhaps more obvious and disturbing is the moment by moment life experience that is plagued with sickness, injury, acts of violence, and other various pains and evils that lead to an unavoidable question. Why? "If we follow the course on which humanity has been led, and become Christians, we then have the 'problem' of pain."[73]

The problem of evil is not just an academic issue. It is also an experiential one. As I write this book, I recall the death of my father. Although he died years ago, there is still a strong feeling of injustice from having watched him suffer for years with kidney failure and dialysis only to die at a young age. His death brought a 21-year-old to a place of emptiness, confusion, and pain that I had not experienced before. I was overwhelmed by it. What made it worse was that I had no answer as to why things had turned out the way they did. Years of church attendance and

---

[72] Francis J. Beckwith, *To Everyone an Answer: A Case for the Christian Worldview: Essays in Honor of Norman L. Geisler* (Downers Grove: InterVarsity Press, 2004), 203.

[73] C. S. Lewis, *The Complete C. S. Lewis Signature Classics* (San Francisco: HarperSanFrancisco, 2002), 379.

casual Christianity had not equipped me for what I was going to experience. This led to my questioning of God's motivations, influence, and love.

C. S. Lewis (1898 - 1963) documents a similar experience in his book *A Grief Observed*.[74] Lewis, one of the most influential theists and philosophers in recent history, worked out this academic issue with clarity in his book, *The Problem of Pain*.[75] However, later in his life, the death of his wife moved him to challenge his own philosophical beliefs. "Don't come talking to me about the consolations of religion or I shall suspect that you don't understand."[76] Lewis wrote, "I not only live each day in grief, but live each day thinking about living each day in grief. Her absence is like the sky, spread over everything. But no, that is not quite accurate. There is one place where her absence comes locally home to me, and it is the place I can't avoid. I mean my own body."[77]

The Faces of Evil

What is Evil? How does one know it when they see it? When does a car or a gun take the step from being a simple mechanical device to something that can be part of a murder? How do we come to understand the devastation and loss of life caused by a hurricane and how is that different from the events that led to the death and destruction the world witnessed on 9-11? It seems clear that there is a difference between a hurricane and an act of terrorism. Although both are evil, one is moral evil and one is natural evil.

"Moral evil is evil brought about by human choices and ac-

---

[74] C. S. Lewis, *A Grief Observed* (San Francisco: Harper & Row, 1961).

[75] C. S. Lewis, *The Problem of Pain* (New York: Macmillan Company, 1944).

[76] Lewis, *The Complete C.S. Lewis Signature Classics*, 449.

[77] Ibid., 445.

tions; any other kind of evil is what we call natural evil."[78] A murder would be considered a moral evil because one person chose to kill another. However, if a person dies in a hurricane, that would be a natural evil because it did not result from the choice and action of a human. A major difference between these two categories is a matter of intent.

If a human chooses to take action that will result in the death of another human, that person has intended to do something that they ought not to do. However, when a person dies in a hurricane, it was not because the hurricane intended to harm the individual. It is simply doing what it ought to do. There is nothing inherently evil about winds going around in a circle extremely fast. Although a hurricane has the potential to cause damage to anything it encounters, it has no intent to do evil.

Regardless of this, evil happens. John Stuart Mill writes: "In sober truth, nearly all the things men are hanged or imprisoned for doing to one another are nature's everyday performance. Killing, the most criminal act recognized by human laws, nature does once to every being that lives, and in a large proportion of cases after protracted tortures such as only the greatest monsters whom we read of ever purposely inflicted on their living fellow creatures."[79]

Tension: Good God, Evil World

Christians hold to a theistic worldview, and there are three attributes of God that, when looked at in combination, seem to be in direct contradiction with the presence of evil in creation. "The problem of evil is grounded on the fact that a number of

---

[78] Francis J. Beckwith, *To Everyone an Answer: A Case for the Christian Worldview: Essays in Honor of Norman L. Geisler* (Downers Grove: InterVarsity Press, 2004), 208.

[79] John Stuart Mill, *Nature, the Utility of Religion, and Theism* (London: Longmans, Green, Reader, and Dryer, 1874), 28.

related and essential beliefs about God appear to be incompatible with the evil we encounter in the world."[80] God of the Bible is described as being infinitely powerful, good, and knowledgeable. However, if God exists, and has the three attributes just mentioned, "He would have both the desire and the power to rid the world of evil."[81] In addition, He would know how to do so.

- God is all-powerful – and can defeat evil.
- God is all-good – and opposes evil.
- God is all-knowing – and foreknew evil.

Omnipotent God

God is omnipotent and has the power to do all things that are in accordance with His character and will. The word *omnipotent* literally means that God is all (*omni*) powerful (*potent*) and is unlimited in ability. Some individuals have argued that God is not all-powerful and is limited in what He can do. One such person is Rabbi Harold Kushner. In his book, *When Bad Things Happen to Good People*, Kushner argues that God is not all-powerful and that is why evil is present in the world.[82]

According to Kushner, God simply does not have the power to do anything about the evil and pain in the world even though He may want to. However, "if this is the case, are we really talking about a God at all or just a finite creature?"[83] The backdrop of Kushner's statements is his painful experience of watching his son die at a young age.

Kushner was not willing to worship a God who had the power to stop his son's suffering and pain and chose not to do so. Kush-

---

[80] Francis J. Beckwith, 207.
[81] Geisler, *The Roots of Evil*, 11.
[82] Harold S. Kushner, *When Bad Things Happen to Good People* (New York: Avon, 1981).
[83] Geisler, *The Roots of Evil*, 27.

ner would consider this a morally deficient God. However, this raises an additional question. What standard is he using to judge God's morality? It would seem that Kushner is using his own personal standard to evaluate God's actions and motivations.

If God must submit to Kushner's standard, or any other, then that standard is bigger than God is and would be God. By judging God's actions, Kushner is taking on the role of God's judge and is now acting as God himself. Kushner suggested that if we can bring ourselves to acknowledge that there are some things God does not control, many good things become possible. He went further to ask if we are capable of forgiving God even when we have found out that He is not perfect?

If God's power is limited, then He is simply not dependable to do what He says He will do, as He may not actually have adequate power for the task. In the case of evil, God would indeed be potentially inadequate to act against it. This would explain the presence of evil in the world. However, Christianity does hold that God is all-powerful, which would include power over evil.

Omnibenevolent God

God is also omnibenevolent. Christians are usually quick to point out that "God is good all the time, and all the time God is good." This is one of the most frequently taught and user-friendly attributes of God in the church today. Everyone desires for God to be a good God that loves them and wants the best for them. Kushner was so passionate about affirming God's goodness that he was willing to sacrifice God's power to affirm it.

Theism asserts that God is not only all-powerful but is also all-good. This is what the word *omni* (all) *benevolent* (good) means. However, if God is really all-good and all-powerful, why does He allow evil and pain to occur in the lives of His creatures? "If the universe is so bad, or even half so bad, how on earth did human beings ever come to attribute it to the activity of a wise and good Creator?"[84]

Some have concluded that God is not really all that good and that He sometimes does things that are unloving. However, "if God is limited in love, He must also be limited in His moral nature. If we are faced with a morally imperfect God, how would we know it?"[85] In other words, in order to judge God's goodness, a standard of goodness must be used.

As stated before, if there is a higher standard of good, then that standard would itself be God. In many cases, that higher standard of good becomes the individual's own preferences and desires. This would certainly seem to be the case in the life of Rabbi Kushner. The truth from a theistic worldview is that "whether we like it or not, God intends to give us what we need, not what we now think we want."[86]

Omniscient God

The attribute of omniscience affirms that God is aware of all things, potential and actual, and that there is absolutely nothing that God does not or cannot know. This is important in the philosophical problem of evil because it indicates that God would indeed have the knowledge of how to defeat evil. He would also know, before He created the world, that evil would be a part of it. An all-knowing God would also be aware of every evil act that an individual was to commit before he or she even committed it.

If this is the case, then why would God not proactively stop every evil act from happening? It seems unlikely that God would know how to deal with evil and choose not to, unless He lacked either the desire or power to prevent and/or remove it. How-

---

[84] Lewis, *The Complete C. S. Lewis Signature Classics*, 374.
[85] Geisler, *The Roots of Evil*, 29.
[86] Lewis, *The Complete C. S. Lewis Signature Classics*, 390.

ever, the theistic God of Christianity is indeed all-good and all-powerful as mentioned above. Therefore, there is an all-powerful, all-good God that also knows everything.

This means that the theistic God of Christianity has the power to defeat evil, the desire to defeat evil, and knows how to defeat evil. From this understanding of God and His attributes comes the philosophical problem of evil. How did evil get here? Why did God allow it? Why does He not destroy it?

CHAPTER 7

THE TRUTH ABOUT EVIL, PART 2

The Three-Part Problem

There are at least three specific problems that flow directly from an understanding of God's omnipotence, omnibenevolence, and omniscience. First, how and why did an all-good God create evil? Second, why does an all-powerful God allow evil to continue? Last, why would God not defeat evil if He has the power, knowledge, and the desire to do it?

1. Did an All-Good God Create Evil?

In Genesis 6, *"the Lord saw that the wickedness of man was great in the earth and that every intent of the thoughts of his heart was on evil continually"* (Genesis 6:5). However, how did this happen? All throughout the creation account in the beginning of Genesis, God affirms that His creation is "good." *"Then God saw everything He had made, and indeed it was very good"* (Genesis 1:31).

What happened between Chapter 1 and Chapter 6 of Genesis? From where did this evil come? How did God's good creation turn out to be evil? The God of the Bible is clearly described as the Creator of all things. Even angels and the heavens are created and are dependent on God for life and existence. There is nothing, other than God, that was not created by God. This is what Genesis is affirming in the creation account; God did it! However, from this understanding of God as Creator, comes a collision with Him as omnibenevolent.

How could God create something that is contrary to His nature and character? Whatever God creates has to be good because He is essentially good, and what flows from Him in the creation process must also be good. However, evil is real and the question is, where did evil come from, if it did not come from God who is the Creator of all things? The following argument is one that might indicate that God is the Creator of evil.

1. God is the Author of everything;
2. Evil is something;
3. Therefore, God is the Author of evil.[87]

This argument is valid, but it is not sound. The second premise, "Evil is something," is incorrect. Evil is not a "thing." For example, darkness is really an absence of light and is therefore not a thing but rather the absence of a thing. This is similar to the relationship between evil and good in that evil relies on good for its very definition.

The analogy of light and dark is still in need of clarification because evil is more than just the absence of good; it is the privation of good. Absence only implies that something is not there. Privation implies that something ought to be present and it is not.

An example that would illustrate the difference between an absence and a privation would be a blind man versus a blind

---

[87] Norman L. Geisler and Ronald M. Brooks, *When Skeptics Ask* (Wheaton: Victor Books, 1990), 60.

rock. In the rock, sight is not expected; therefore, blindness would be an absence of sight. However, for the man, sight is expected; therefore, the blindness is a privation of sight. "Evil exists in a good thing as a lack or imperfection in it, like a hole in a piece of wood."[88] To say that evil is a "thing" is not true.

It also follows that the conclusion that God authored evil based on it being something is also not true. Everything that God created was good at the point of creation. Although God is not the Creator of evil, He is the Creator of the good creatures that choose to do evil. God created a world in which evil was possible, but it was creatures that made evil actual by choosing things that were not good. "He created the **fact of freedom**; we perform the **acts of freedom**. He made evil possible; men made evil actual."[89]

Did God make a mistake? NO, we did!

2. Why Does God Allow Evil To Continue?

Why does God allow evil to continue? Because God is omniscient, He would have known that men would choose to do evil. Specifically, He must have known that Adam and Eve would be disobedient in the garden and that evil would be the result. So, why did God allow this to happen? Even if God is not the author of evil, it would seem that His omnipotence would allow Him to keep evil from happening through either a miraculous event or other preventative measures.

Why could God not have blown a great wind that made it impossible for Eve to get to the fruit she was tempted to eat? It seems that God could also miraculously turn a gun into a banana just before a murder happens. Could God have stopped the events of 9-11 by causing each of the terrorists to have a spontaneous heart attack before they killed thousands of people?

---

[88] Geisler, *The Roots of Evil*, 20.
[89] Geisler and Brooks, *When Skeptics Ask*, 62.

How many people have prayed to God for healing when they hear the words, "You have cancer," yet have died anyway? "We can, perhaps, conceive of a world in which God corrected the results of this abuse of free will by His creatures at every moment … but such a world would be one in which wrong actions were impossible, and in which, therefore, freedom of the will would be void."[90]

Understanding of why God allows evil to continue begins with a proper understanding of free will and the fall of man. Free will is one of the "good" things that God created. "Free will means the ability to make an unforced decision between two or more alternatives."[91] There is nothing evil about free will, but a person can use the free will God gives him to make choices that are contrary to God's will. What if God prevented every evil act from happening? God can't stop all evil acts without destroying all freedom to choose between good and evil, which would remove free will.

In God's sovereignty, He gave man free will. Knowing that this act would lead to the fall of man, the death of His Son on the cross, and the suffering of many people spending eternity in Hell, could God have just not given man free will? At first, this option makes sense. However, the only way for God to allow love to be shared between a creature and a Creator is for both to choose to participate in the relationship.

Love cannot be forced, because forced love is really rape. If there is the potential for a person to choose to have a relationship with God, it would follow that the potential for man not to choose God would also have to be real. This is why God allowed for the possibility of evil and why free will is a good thing for

---

[90] Lewis, *The Complete C. S. Lewis Signature Classics*, 382.
[91] Geisler and Brooks, *When Skeptics Ask*, 63.

Him to have created. It was the only way for man to have the potential to love God.

Why does God allow evil? If He didn't, there would be no freedom to choose good. In God's sovereignty, He gave us free will. Evil exists in our world as a direct result of man's abuse of free will. Free will was part of God's good and perfect creation. However, since the time of Adam and Eve, humanity has chosen to use it for selfish motivations.

3. Why does God not Conquer Evil?

C. S. Lewis noted that God must be terribly offended at our behavior. He writes, "We actually are, at present, creatures whose character must be, in some respects, a horror to God as it is, when we really see it, a horror to ourselves. This I believe to be a fact: and I notice that the holier a man is, the more fully he is aware of this fact."[92] Why does an all-good and all-powerful God not just destroy evil and remove it from the world? "The classic form of this argument has been rattling through the halls of college campuses for hundreds of years."[93]

1. If God is all-good, He would destroy evil.

2. If God is all-powerful, He could destroy evil.

3. But evil is not destroyed.

4. Hence, there is no such God.[94]

This argument is valid and seems to stop the theist from being able to fully deal with the problem of evil. However, it is not true because it leaves out one crucial word: *yet.* Just because God has not yet defeated evil, this does not mean that evil will not be defeated or destroyed by God in the future. In fact, the argument

---

[92] Ibid., 396.
[93] Geisler and Brooks, *When Skeptics Ask*, 63.
[94] Ibid.

seems to boomerang on itself and point to the absolute necessity of God to one day deal with evil. Instead of working against the theist worldview, this line of thinking actually works to support it, predicting what God's response to the evil and pain in the world will be. "Since we have not yet finished with history, it is possible that all evil in history will one day cease."[95]

In fact, the only way to refute the potential for God to one day destroy evil would be to see all of time, which only an infinite being could do. One would actually have to be God to have a vantage point that could affirm or deny that evil will be dealt with sometime in the future. Even Rabbi Kushner admits that he would believe in an all-powerful God if and when he witnessed God's righteous judgment and defeat over the evils of this world.

Of course, it is not a difficult task to find biblical support for both the official defeat of evil and the actual defeat of evil. Christ's victory over the grave was the first part of God's work to defeat the evil in the world:

"Having wiped out the handwriting of requirements that was against us, which was contrary to us. And He has taken it out of the way, having nailed it to the cross. Having disarmed principalities and powers, He made a public spectacle of them, triumphing over them in it" (Colossians 2:14-15).

"Inasmuch then as the children have partaken of flesh and blood, He Himself likewise shared in the same, that through death He might destroy him who had the power of death, that is, the devil, and release those who through fear of death were all their lifetime subject to bondage" (Hebrews 2:14-15).

The book of Revelation points toward the actual completion of this work as Christ finally deals with Satan and the evil of the world.

---

[95] Geisler, *The Roots of Evil*, 35.

"Now I saw heaven opened, and behold, a white horse. And He who sat on him was called Faithful and True, and in righteousness He judges and makes war. His eyes were like a flame of fire, and on His head were many crowns. He had a name written that no one knew except Himself. He was clothed with a robe dipped in blood, and His name is called The Word of God. And the armies in heaven, clothed in fine linen, white and clean, followed Him on white horses. Now out of His mouth goes a sharp sword, that with it He should strike the nations. And He Himself will rule them with a rod of iron. He Himself treads the winepress of the fierceness and wrath of Almighty God" (Revelation 19:11-15).

"And God will wipe every tear from their eye; there shall be no more death, nor sorrow, nor crying. There shall be no more pain, for the former things have passed away" (Revelation 21:4).

Because God has not yet removed evil, we live in an evil world that results in pain and suffering. The argument that was stated above should be altered to the following:

1. If God is all-good, He will defeat evil.

2. If God is all-powerful, He can defeat evil.

3. Evil is not *yet* defeated.

4. Therefore, God can and *will one day* defeat evil.[96]

The analogy of a symphony orchestra works well to illustrate this point. Imagine that the entire universe is a philharmonic orchestra in concert, we might designate certain objects as instruments. A series of events or an era in history might then represent a particular movement within the overall concert. The death of an innocent man during this era might be represented by a dissonant chord and the Second World War by several measures of the score. If the symphony had been playing for thousands of

---

[96] Geisler and Brooks, *When Skeptics Ask*, 64.

years and someone listened to only a few minutes of the very dissonant section, he would not be fair in pronouncing the whole symphony "horrible" or the dissonant part "unjustified." In the same way, it may be that there are some examples of suffering that do not seem justified from our vantage point, but these may nevertheless be ultimately justified.[97]

God CAN and WILL one day defeat evil.

---

[97] Geisler, *The Roots of Evil*, 37.

CHAPTER 8

THE TRUTH ABOUT EVIL, PART 3

ALREADY...BUT NOT YET

Although we are already children of God, we have not yet experienced the fullness of our salvation. Through faith, we are now God's children but when Jesus appears we will become like Him. As we keep His promise of transformation in view, and fix our desire on the goal of perfection, we will grow in purity here and now. There are three aspects to the process of our salvation.

Justification-salvation is freedom from the *penalty* of sin and is a movement from death to life. When we believe in Jesus Christ for eternal life we experience justification. Paul makes it clear in Ephesians 2:8-9 that justification is experienced by the grace of God through faith in Christ. Faith alone in Christ alone is the cause of our salvation from death to eternal life. It is not the STRENGTH of our faith but the OBJECT of our faith that gives us victory.

Second, once we are alive in Christ, we begin the ongoing process of sanctification. Sanctification-salvation is being freed from the *power* of sin in our lives. This ongoing transformation causes us to be more like Christ.

Last, every Christian can look forward to glorification. Glorification-salvation is freedom from the very *presence* of sin and is the ultimate state of every believer. Think about how wonderful it will be to see Jesus and to be free of all the sinful and fallen aspects of this world and our flesh.

As Christians, we have an amazing future ahead of us. Experiencing new life through faith in Christ is truly overwhelming, but the best is yet to come. Paul wrote about this to the church in Philippi: "*But our citizenship is in heaven, and from it we await a Savior, the Lord Jesus Christ, who will transform our lowly body to be like His glorious body, by the power that enables Him even to subject all things to Himself*" (Philippians 3:20-21 ESV).

This is not supposed to be the best of all possible worlds. This is the best of all possible ways to the best of all possible worlds. When you go through difficult times, remember that God is at work and He never wastes a hurt. His silence is not absence. Sometimes waiting is important, so be prepared to be still and have hope. Realize you are not alone and the journey is important. Our freedom from pain is delayed but not denied. Jesus is enough. Ask yourself … what is God doing here? Ask yourself … will I trust Him?

"*The Lord is my rock and my fortress and my deliverer; My God, my strength, in whom I will trust; My shield and the horn of my salvation, my stronghold*" (Psalm 18:2).

GREATER THAN

"*Little children, you are from God and have overcome them, for He Who is in you is greater than he who is in the world*" (1 John 4:4, ESV).

Pro wrestling is staged. Before the wrestlers go out, it has been predetermined who will win. The contenders go through the battle for entertainment purposes. The point of the battle is not to decide who will win, but to give the crowd a show. The winner of the match does not battle **for** victory but **from** victory. He battles knowing that he has already won.

Those who believe in Jesus Christ for eternal life have already won but have not yet finished fighting. God allows us to go through our Christian walk, not to win the victory but to show off to the world that, He that is in us is greater than he that is in the world.

Relying on God is the secret to all spiritual victory in our lives. The Holy Spirit is greater than Satan and even greater than our own hearts. We overcome evil as He gives us strength to resist temptations to doubt, deny, disregard, and disobey the Word of God.

We don't fight FOR victory … we fight FROM victory.

WHAT HAPPENS AFTER WE DIE?

The Bema Seat of Christ and The Great White Throne of Judgment are the two major judgments mentioned in the Bible. The Great White Throne of Judgment is for unbelievers and the Bema (Judgment) Seat of Christ is for believers. As believers, we do not have to fear judgment of our sins because Christ took our judgment upon Himself at the cross. OUR SERVICE will be evaluated at the judgment seat of Christ, not OUR SIN.

When we stand before Him, it will be for **REWARD** not **REPRIMAND**. The Crown of Righteousness, the Crown of Life, the Incorruptible Crown, the Crown of Rejoicing, and the Crown of Glory are five of the crowns of reward mentioned in the New Testament. Unlike the rewards we receive in life, the rewards we receive at the Judgment Seat of Christ are eternal and will never perish.

Our judgment will be for **REWARD** not **REPRIMAND**.

BIBLICAL RESPONSE TO EVIL

God is yet to destroy evil. However, Christians can have assurance that God wants to remove evil, knows how to remove evil, and has the power to remove evil. God will remove evil from the presence of His people in the new Heaven and new Earth. "This fallen world is not the best possible world, but it is the best way to obtain the best possible world."[98] Perhaps this is what Paul meant when he said, *"For I consider that the sufferings of this present time are not worthy to be compared with the glory which shall be revealed in us."* (Romans 8:18).

There are a number of verses that specifically deal with how we should respond to the pain and evil that we encounter in this life:

"Yea, though I walk through the valley of the shadow of death, I will fear no evil; For You are with me; Your rod and Your staff, they comfort me" (Psalm 23:4).

"My brethren, count it all joy when you fall into various trials, knowing that the testing of your faith produces patience. But let patience have its perfect work, that you may be perfect and complete, lacking nothing" (James 1:2-4).

"And we know that all things work together for good to those who love God, to those who are the called according to His purpose" (Romans 8:28).

"Beloved, do not think it strange concerning the fiery trial which is to try you, as though some strange thing happened to you; but rejoice to the extent that you partake of Christ's sufferings, that when His glory is revealed, you may also be glad with exceeding joy" (1 Peter 4:12-13).

"In this you greatly rejoice, though now for a little while, if need be, you have been grieved by various trials, that the genuineness of your faith, being much more precious than gold that perishes, though it is tested by fire, may be found to praise, honor, and glory at the

---

[98] Geisler, *The Roots of Evil*, 59.

revelation of Jesus Christ" (1 Peter 1:6-7).

"And not only that, but we also glory in tribulations, knowing that tribulation produces perseverance; and perseverance, character; and character, hope. Now hope does not disappoint, because the love of God has been poured out in our hearts by the Holy Spirit who was given to us" (Romans 5:3-5).

It seems clear from these verses that God not only acknowledges our pain but also wants to help in times of pain and trouble. As believers, we should not be afraid of suffering. Instead, we should rejoice because God is going to work out something good because of it. Despite the fact that He is not the cause of evil, He is active in our lives to use evil for good.

C. S. Lewis wrote that "God whispers to us in our pleasures, speaks to us in our conscience, but shouts in our pains: it is His megaphone to rouse a deaf world."[99] **God never wastes a hurt.** An individual's response is what determines whether that person becomes **better** or **bitter** when pain comes his way.

Perhaps we are allowed to suffer because God is much more concerned with our **character** than He is with our **comfort**. "But you cannot argue backward and link someone's specific pain to a direct act of God."[100] That being said, God is more concerned with our response to pain than He is with our understanding of the cause of pain. This can be seen in the case studies that follow.

CASE STUDY: JOB

The book of Job is perhaps the earliest writing in the Bible. Job was one of the most faithful men of his time, and yet God allowed Satan to destroy his possessions, family, and eventually his health. Although Job did not die, he was physically, emotionally,

---

[99] Lewis, *The Complete C.S. Lewis Signature Classics*, 406.
[100] Philip Yancey, *Where Is God When It Hurts* (Grand Rapids: Zondervan, 1990), 92.

and spiritually tested.

Toward the end of the book of Job, God and Job dialogue about the suffering that Job has experienced. As one might imagine, Job asks God why He has allowed this to happen to him. "God's reply to Job comprises one of His longest single speeches in the Bible, and because it appears at the end of the Bible's most complete treatise on suffering it merits a close-up look."[101]

God's response seems to ignore Job's question of why and instead points him to what his proper response to the events in his life should be. Job stayed true to his faith in God and worshiped Him in the midst of a horribly painful time in his life. He also acknowledged that God was using this for good when he said, *"But He knows the way that I take; When He has tested me, I shall come forth as gold"* (Job 23:10).

In the end, Job was given more than was taken away; "Now the LORD blessed the latter days of Job more than his beginning…" (Job 42:12). This serves as a picture of how God will make right all of our suffering when this life is over.

CASE STUDY: JESUS

The teachings and work of Christ also deal with the problem of evil and pain. One example of this is the man born blind in John 9. Jesus is asked why the man has been born blind and responds that it glorifies God. This, as in Job, points to the proper response to the pain rather than answers the question asked of Jesus. "Sometimes, as with the man born blind, the work of God is manifest through a dramatic miracle. Sometimes it is not. But in every case, suffering offers an opportunity for us to display God's work."[102]

---

[101] Ibid., 111-112.
[102] Ibid., 93.

Jesus also taught that the greatest love possible is achieved when a person suffers death. *"Greater love has no one than this, than to lay down one's life for his friends"* (John 15:13). The writer of Hebrews gives an account of this act of greatest love by Christ; *"Looking unto Jesus, the author and finisher of our faith, who for the joy that was set before Him endured the cross, despising the shame, and has sat down at the right hand of the throne of God"* (Hebrews 12:2). Christ's work on the cross was no doubt overwhelmingly painful as was His suffering when He took on the sinfulness of the world. Through His suffering, we are made alive. *"For as in Adam all die, even so in Christ all shall be made alive"* (1 Corinthians 15:22).

GOD'S GREAT LOVE

Through faith, we are now God's children and He is our loving Father. One of the problems we encounter when we address the subject of love is that there are many different definitions of the word love. In the time of the writing of the Scriptures, there were **four different words** that were used to define "love."

1. Agape - Godly love

2. Phileo - Brotherly love

3. Eros - Erotic love

4. Storge - Family or affectionate love

One of the reasons things may seem "out of focus" in the lives of many Christians is that we do not have a clear understanding of **AGAPE LOVE**.

Agape Love Is:

1. The highest kind of love

2. Characterized by sacrifice

3. Biblically equated with God – spiritual and divine

4. One of the most common words within the text of the New Testament

5. One of the rarest words in Greek writing and almost impossible to find apart from the New Testament

6. The power that moves us to respond to someone else's needs with no expectation of reward

7. The willingness to give of one's self totally, with abandon, for the one who is the object of our love

8. From God alone and best personified in Jesus Christ

9. The answer to the yearnings in the hearts of those who have known only selfish love

10. A matter of the will, not emotion

THOUGHTS ON THE FALL

As has been shown, all things that God created, including free will to make choices, were good. "Our present condition, then, is explained by the fact that we are members of a spoiled species."[103] This "fall" of man is the source of much discussion.

C. S. Lewis said the following about the fall: "The story in Genesis is a story (full of the deepest suggestion) about a magic apple of knowledge; but in the developed doctrine the inherent magic of the apple has quite dropped out of sight, and the story is simply one of disobedience. I have the deepest respect even for the Pagan myths, still more for myths in Holy Scripture. I therefore do not doubt that the version which emphasizes the magic apple, and brings together the trees of life and knowledge, contains a deeper and subtler truth than the version which makes

---

[103] Lewis, *The Complete C. S. Lewis Signature Classics*, 403.

the apple simply and solely a pledge of obedience."[104]

THOUGHTS ON HELL

Only one of two terminal options is present for the theist. Either a person is to spend an eternity in Heaven or an eternity in Hell. This brings up an additional question of why an all-good God would send someone to Hell. It is clear in the Gospel of John that God does not will men into Hell. Man wills himself into Hell.

In his book, *The Great Divorce*, C. S. Lewis wrote, "There are only two kinds of people in the end: those who say to God, 'Thy will be done,' and those to whom God says, in the end 'Thy will be done.' All that are in Hell, choose it. Without that self-choice there could be no Hell. "

"He who believes in Him is not condemned; but he who does not believe is condemned already, because he has not believed in the name of the only begotten Son of God" (John 3:18).

"He who believes in the Son has everlasting life; and he who does not believe the Son shall not see life, but the wrath of God abides on him" (John 3:36).

"He who rejects Me, and does not receive My words, has that which judges him—the word that I have spoken will judge him in the last day" (John 12:48).

"You search the Scriptures, for in them you think you have eternal life; and these are they which testify of Me. But you are not willing to come to Me that you may have life" (John 5:39-40).

WANT VS. WILL

Of course, no one, when asked if they want to go to Hell, would say, "Yeah, I would love to." Hell is a place of eternal sepa-

---

[104] Ibid., 398.

ration from an all-good and all-powerful God and is described as a place of never-ending suffering. There is absolutely nothing about Hell, as described in the Bible, which would cause a person to want to go there.

However, the unbeliever wills his or herself into Hell and locks the door from the inside. In contrast to this, Heaven is described as a place where pain and evil are no longer experienced. "Scripture and tradition habitually put the joys of heaven into the scale against the suffering of earth, and no solution of the problem of pain which does not do so can be called a Christian one."[105]

The person who spends eternity in Heaven will finally be free from not only the power of sin but also its presence. In Heaven, it will no longer be possible for a person to will to do evil. Although that sounds like a loss of freedom or free will, it is not. Freedom is not the ability to do otherwise; it is the ability to activate self-determined acts. By placing one's faith in Christ for eternal life, a person is activating a self-determining act. This act ensures that the believer will one day have sin taken away when in Heaven.

SUMMARY

Anyone who decides to adopt a theist worldview must think through the problem of pain. This philosophic problem is one of the main issues that hinder intellectual thinkers from believing in God. They look around at our world, see all the pain, suffering, and injustice, and reject the potential for an all-loving, all-powerful God. As apologists, we simply must love people enough to be ready to answer the hard questions. Peter instructs us to *"Always be ready to give a defense to everyone who asks you a reason for the hope that is in you"* (1 Peter 3:15).

---

[105] Lewis, *The Complete C. S. Lewis Signature Classics*, 427.

REVIEW OF OBJECTIVES

PART ONE: THE BIG CONCEPTS

1. **Define Christian apologetics.**
   - The defense of the Christian faith.
2. **Explain why Christian apologetics is important.**
   - Reason demands it and the Bible commands it.
3. **Define *truth*.**
   - Telling it like it is.
4. **Evaluate this statement: "Christianity is true for you but not for me."**
   - Absolute truth is true for all people in all times and all places.
5. **Defend this statement: "The Bible is wholly true in all it affirms."**
   - Jesus is the key.
   - Jesus claimed and proved to be God by:
     - Fulfilling prophecy
     - Living a sinless and miraculous life
     - Predicting and accomplishing His resurrection from the dead
   - If Jesus is God, then anything He teaches is true.
   - Jesus affirmed the scope of the Old Testament and promised the divine authority of the New Testament.

- Evidence for the reliability of the manuscripts:
  - Number of New Testament Manuscripts
  - Early dates of the New Testament
  - Accuracy of the New Testament Manuscripts
  - Confirmation by early fathers

6. **List three reasons, other than the Bible, why we know God exists.**
   - Cosmological Argument: Anything that has a beginning has a beginner.
   - Teleological Argument: Anything that has a design has a designer.
   - Moral Argument: If there is a moral law, there must be a moral lawgiver.

7. **List the three major worldviews.**
   - Theism
   - Atheism
   - Pantheism

8. **Explain how we understand Jesus is God.**
   - Jesus was both fully God and fully man.

9. **Explain why this statement is false: "Christians claim they worship one God, but they actually worship three: Jesus, the Holy Spirit, and God the Father."**
   - God is one What and three Whos in the same way a triangle has three sides but is only one triangle.

10. **Define** *miracle*.

- A special act of God that interrupts the natural course of events.

11. List three reasons miracles are critical to Christianity.

- To glorify the nature of God.
- To accredit certain persons as the spokespeople for God.
- To provide evidence for belief in God.

PART TWO: THE BIG CONTENDERS

12. Describe three characteristics of a world religion.

- Usually has an origin completely independent of Christianity.
- Usually has little in common doctrinally with Christianity.
- Often considers itself the only true religion.

13. List the four major world religions.

- Christianity
- Islam
- Hinduism
- Buddhism

14. From a Christian perspective, define cult.

- Any group with false religious teachings, other than a world religion, that stands in opposition to the historic, orthodox Christian faith.
- Usually an offshoot of Christianity.
- Denies one or more of the doctrines of historic Christianity.
- Often considers itself the only true expression of Christianity.

15. Describe three ways cults differ from Christianity.

- An extra-scriptural source of authority.
- The denial of justification by faith alone.
- The devaluation of Jesus Christ and His uniqueness.

16. Explain the differences between a world religion and a cult.

- World Religion: different god.
- Cult: different doctrine.

PART THREE: THE BIG CRITICISM

17. **Answer this question: "If God is good, why did He create evil?"**

    - God did not create evil because evil is not a thing.
    - Evil is the privation of some good thing that should be there.
    - God created freewill, which is a good thing.
    - God created the fact of freedom; we perform the acts of freedom.
    - God made evil possible; we made evil actual.

18. **Explain why God allows painful things to happen.**

    - If He didn't, there would be no freedom to choose good.

19. **Explain how you would answer a friend who asked you to give a Christian answer to this argument: If God is all-good, He would destroy evil. If God is all-powerful, He could destroy evil. But evil is not destroyed. Therefore, there is no such God.**

    - The argument is missing the word "YET".
    - God will destroy all evil. He has simply not done it YET.
      - If God is all-good, He will defeat evil.
      - If God is all-powerful, He can defeat evil.
      - Evil is not **yet** defeated.
      - Therefore, God can and will one day defeat evil.

Steve Gaines

Believers who read the New Testament often come away with the conviction that there must be more to following Christ than what they are experiencing. In this Amazon best seller, Steve Gaines points out that the glaring disconnect between modern Christianity and that of the first century is not due to deficiencies in our sermons or our singing. The problem is our praying.

Jim Richards

In today's ever changing culture, Christians need encouragement to respond to the pressures assaulting our faith. In this book believers see how to have victory in Jesus by having a godly attitude while facing trials and challenges.

Steve Gaines

Have you ever been so excited about something that you had to share it with others? That's the way it should be with every Christian. We should be so enthusiastic about the fact that Jesus is our Lord and Savior that we cannot contain the good news. Learn how to politely, scripturally, effectively, and easily share the gospel of Jesus Christ.

For teaching guides and additional small group study materials, or to learn about other Auxano Press titles, visit Auxanopress.com.

Other Books
by Ken Hemphill

Do you believe God's truth is more precious than gold? Do you dig into God's Word with the same passion you would exert to find physical gold? Learn three different styles of reading and eight essential questions to ask of every text to help you discover the pure riches of God's Word.

This study of the love, atonement, and mission of God addresses the crucial issue of the extent of the gospel and who can respond to the good news. It will encourage every person to confidently join Unlimited God in His Kingdom mission to redeem the peoples of the whole world.

For teaching guides and additional small group study materials, or to learn about other Auxano Press titles, visit Auxanopress.com.

Auxano Press Non-Disposable Curriculum

- Designed for use in any small group
- Affordable, biblically based, and life oriented
- Choose your own material and stop and start times
- Study the Bible and build a Christian library

Auxano
PRESS

For teaching guides and additional small group study materials, or to learn about other Auxano Press titles, visit Auxanopress.com.